Prayer Secrets

Guy H. King

All Scripture quotations are from the *King James Version* (KJV) of the Bible.

PRAYER SECRETS

ISBN 13: 978-0-9428-8911-6
ISBN: 0-942889-11-8
Printed in the United States of America
Copyright © 1997 by Christ Life Publications
Reprinted © 2011

Christ Life Publications
P.O. Box 399
Vinton, Virginia 24179

Preface

Never has there been a day when prayer was a more significant topic for the Church, for the believer. Greater pressures, greater temptations, and greater opportunities have never faced any generation before us.

While there seems to be much prayer made in our day, there seems to be little to show for it many times. Perhaps we have lost or left some of the determining elements that make for prayer that moves Heaven.

In this classic book, Guy H. King addresses in simple, yet profound style, a number of facets of effectual, fervent prayer. This work seems to be a source document. Preachers across America have quoted from it in their preaching and writing (perhaps unknowingly) for years. Its reprinting will prove a great impetus to the kind of prayer so lacking in our times.

The work has been edited to remove British spellings and the use of Roman numerals. Sentence structure has been simplified somewhat to improve readability. However, care has been taken to preserve both the general style and the complete content of the writer.

As you read, you will notice several references to "Keswick" or "Keswick Convention." Those unfamiliar with this movement should know that it was a revival movement which had its roots in England around 1870. Of further historical interest is an illustration mentioning Lord Nuffield (1877-1963), a wealthy British motor manufacturer and benefactor.

May our Lord use this fine work to *"teach us to pray."*

Table of Contents

1

The Invitation

"Ask . . . seek . . . knock" —Luke 11:9

We are setting out to think over, talk over, and take over some of the Secrets of Prayer that are disclosed to reverent inquirers in God's Book. Prayer should occupy a very large place in a Christian's life, even as it did in that of his Master. Prayer, rightly used, is a tremendous force in the world. It behooves us, therefore, to find out all we can about its secrets. Let us, then, by a definite act of will, and in a real attitude of worship, seek to learn His mind upon this great and holy theme. The text introduces us to what is the first of the Secrets—The Invitation.

God Makes The First Move

It is as well to learn at the very outset that, first, prayer is not forcing our way into God's presence, but that He has invited us to come in. We never could intrude upon Him. Everything turns upon His gracious willingness to admit us. How reassuring, therefore, that He bids us come and "Ask." We note also that, second, prayer is not wringing something from a reluctant God. On the contrary, He is "always more ready to hear than we to pray, and...

wont to give more than either we desire or deserve." It is, further, not unimportant to observe that, third, prayer is not a breaking in upon the laws of God's universe. Prayer is itself one of those laws. Scorn is sometimes poured upon the objective efficacy of our intercession, because the universe is governed according to the rule of Law. But every law works in with all other laws, and prayer is one of those laws. God has said, "If ye ask . . . I will do . . ." (John 14:14), thus coupling law and effect together. He has taken the initiative, and has invited us to "Ask."

The Next Move is Ours

It is for us now to accept the wondrous invitation. Yet, how slow we are to do so. Our bodies get tired, our spirits get jaded, our minds get preoccupied, our hearts get lukewarm. So often there is a little alacrity about our prayer life. Strange way to treat a Royal Invitation, isn't it? He makes an appointment to meet us at The Throne of Grace, and too often we fail to keep the appointment. Moreover, how quick we are to give up. A very little delay in the expected answer is enough to cause most of us to grow weary and disappointed. Yet, in the terms of His invitation, He has warned us that the answer will not necessarily come at once. Asking is, in that case, to be succeeded by seeking; and that should, if necessary, be followed by knocking. The Master has told us in this passage that prayer is like a needy man going to a friend's house for help. Arriving at the gate, this man may call out to his friend, and Ask for what he wants.

But if he gets no reply, he may make his way round the house, and Seek for his friend, that he may explain his need. And if that will not satisfy, he may go to his door, and Knock until at last he is answered. So does the Lord invite us, not only to pray, but to persevere. The tense of the Greek words justifies us translating as "Keep on asking, keep on seeking, keep on knocking."

The Last Move is God's Again

When we have breathed our prayer, that is not the end of the matter, as if there were no other answer to prayer than a subjective one—that is, the happy and healthful influence that it has upon our own soul. Let the multitudinous promises of God's Word, and the multifarious experiences of man's life combine to assure us that prayer has objective results as well. Prayer changes things, and prayer gets things. He will not fail the suppliant. His specific word to him is, "Ye shall have"—not always the thing you asked for, but if not that, something you need more. But always something. And He will not fool the suppliant. He does not invite him to "ask" in order that He may mock him. If he ask for bread, He will not give him a stone. Sometimes, instead of bread, he may be joyously surprised to eat cake—but never a stone. Ah yes, when he comes for "water" (Isaiah 55:1), he may often get "wine and milk"!

That is how it is in prayer—our side, and His side, our move, and His move. You remember Jacob's Ladder. The angels of God were "ascending" and "descending" on it (Genesis 28:12)—as if going up with his needs, and coming down with God's supplies; his prayers moving up, His answers moving down. Was Jacob's, then, the first move after all? No. God moved first, when He put the ladder there!

This then, is our first Prayer Secret. The realization of the precious truth will make such a difference—when you come into the Presence of God to pray, you are there by Invitation! The Master has a way of issuing His invitations in a very widespread manner. A little child is bidden to come and lispingly "ask" his simple petitions. An aged saint is encouraged to come and patiently "seek" the grace and blessing he desires. Even a sinner is allowed to come and urgently "knock" for one thing: the Bread of Life, the Water of Life. Let no one then hesitate to accept the gracious Invitation on the ground of a realization of deep unworthiness. Of course, we are not worthy to come. We all know that. God knows that better than we do. Yet, in spite of it He bids us come, without fear, without hesitation, without doubt. He has arranged a plan for meeting that unworthiness—but that is another of our Prayer Secrets.

2

The Presence

"There am I"—Matthew 18:20

No simpler words could be found in all the dictionary. No profounder truth could be found in all the language. Apart from everything else, we have here one of the greatest of all the Prayer Secrets. We have received and personally answered the Invitation. Now we are to consider the Presence into which we have been ushered. Let us examine each of the beautiful monosyllables that the text brings before us.

The Adverb

"There." Where? The context quite precisely answers our question. It says, "Where two or three are gathered together in My Name."

The Company

We have here, first, the company—be it but "two or three." There are Christians who choose to despise the assemblies of God's people. They can get along quite well without going to church, and so on. Yet their Master showed a particular interest in, and concern for, the gatherings of His disciples, as, for example, in the Upper Room on the first Easter evening. Moreover, the keenest of the early believers were accounted praiseworthy for "not forsaking the assembling of ourselves together, as the manner of some is . . . and so much more as ye see the day approaching" (Hebrews 10:25). Here in our passage a special promise, and a special blessing, are guaranteed to the assembly. Make no mistake about it, the companies of saints are very precious in His eyes, and should be so in ours as well.

The Bond

Here also is, second, the bond —"in My Name." James 2:7 speaks of "that worthy Name by the which ye are called." The company may be a very varied assortment. There may be among them old and young, clever and dull, distinguished and ordinary, rich and poor—but they all bear the Name. They are fellow–partners in the same business, fellow–members of the same family, fellow–soldiers in the same army. "Blest be the tie that binds our hearts in Christian love." When any such, however few, gather together, it is their Lord's delight to be "There"!

The Pronoun

"I." And who is this? We might take up the whole of the rest of this volume in considering that Person. But it must suffice to pick out only a few things for emphasis.

The Living One

He is, of course, the Living One—not just a great

historical figure, not just a spiritual influence, not just a beautiful, fond memory. When we enter the Presence, we meet One Who is gloriously alive! The comprehension of that can completely transform and even electrify our prayer time.

The Holy One

He is also the Holy One. The blessed communion with Himself that He so graciously permits His children will never for a moment dim the sense of His absolute, awe-inspiring holiness. The nearer we approach to Him, the more intimate our fellowship becomes, the more utterly appropriate will it seem that we should "put off thy shoes from off thy feet, for the place whereon thou standest is holy ground" (Exodus 3:5). We wonder how ever such as we can come into the Presence of such as He. Only a most wonderful provision can make access possible, as a later Secret will reveal. A remembrance of this point will save us from rushing unthinkingly to prayer, and from an undue familiarity with words.

The Almighty One

Then, too, is He the Almighty One—"able to do exceeding abundantly above all that we ask or think" of asking (Ephesians 3:20). You can't bring a request too big for Him. You can't bring a problem too hard for Him. When He introduced Himself to Abram as "the Almighty God" (Genesis 17:1), the Name He chose was El-Shaddai. The significance of that word is "The God Who is Enough"—great enough, wise enough, tender enough, understanding enough, powerful enough for anything that you can ever bring to Him! This, then, is something of the nature of the One Whose presence we are allowed to enjoy when we come together to pray. Will not these qualities make a difference to us as we come?

The Verb

"Am"—the little word demands our close attention.

Its Importance

Its importance lies in the fact that it is an unequivocal statement of the case. The thing is true apart altogether from our comprehension or realization of it. You remember Jacob's testimony, "Surely the Lord is in this place, and I knew it not" (Genesis 28:16). It was a pity that he did not know it, but his ignorance did not alter the fact. Our verb is just another clear assertion of the same truth.

Its Significance

Its significance lies in the fact that it is a present tense, not a future tense. This seems to indicate that it is not a promise, but a statement. It is not, "There will I be," as if, when we are gathered, He will come and join us (which were a beautiful thought). Rather, it is "There am I," as if He were there first, and when we gather in His Name, we find He is there before us at the place of appointment. He is there to welcome us, one by one, as we come!

The Presence—what a Prayer Secret it is! And let us not forget how almost all that we have said applies to the individual prayer time, as well as to the prayer meeting. In both cases, the Sense of the Presence means so much.

"God is here!"

3

The Threshold

"By the Blood of Jesus"—Hebrews 10:19

We will be careful not to use the word "Blood" crudely in this connection. We will speak it with reverence and with wonder. We will write it with a capital. For it is "precious" as 1 Peter 1:19 reminds us. This means not only that it is highly esteemed among us, but primarily that it is of infinite value in the eyes of God. Certainly we ourselves can never gauge what we owe to that outpouring of atoning and redeeming love.

We Cannot Survive Without the Blood

Some have tried to dispense with it, but only to their own undoing.

The Red Strain is to be Seen

All Through Scripture

It speaks from Genesis to Revelation—typically, prophetically, and actually—of the Blood of the Lamb. Large tracts of the Bible remain unintelligible unless, and until, that fact is recognized.

Why the Sacrifice of Cain Was Rejected

Cain's sacrifice was rejected because there was no Blood in it! Doubtless it was excellent in its own way, but it was not God's way. He had ordained that the sin offering should be of Blood, because it was the type of, and was the temporary expedient awaiting, and therefore drew its own efficacy from, the One Offering to be Once for all made in God's good time.

Much Preaching Falls Short

Preaching may be exceedingly clever; it may become extremely popular. But it has no real saving quality if it has omitted "the Blood," in all its New Testament significance.

We Cannot Escape Without the Blood

We are by nature more terribly in bondage than were the children of Israel in Egypt. Their glorious deliverance is the Divinely–intended picture of the only way in which we can be freed from our thralldom to sin.

The Power of Redemption is God's Grace

They were so utterly enslaved that they could not raise a finger to save themselves, any more than we sinners can find an escape in our own good deeds, or in our own strong resolutions. "By grace are ye saved through faith . . . not of works" (Ephesians 2:8, 9). How well we know the blessed truth.

The Price of Redemption Was

Pictured in the Passover Lamb

It is ". . . a lamb . . . the lamb . . . your lamb," as it is so significantly described in Exodus 12:3, 4, and 5, and whose sprinkled Blood speaks to us so movingly of "the Blood of sprinkling" (Hebrews 12:24). It is only because "Christ our Passover is sacrificed for us," as 1 Corinthians 5:7 tells us, that we are able to make our exodus from our Egypt of sin, and our entrance into our Canaan of full salvation.

We Cannot Get in Without the Blood

Into Heaven Hereafter

The Glory is open to every Blood–washed soul, and it is closed to all whose hearts remain unsprinkled.

Into the Holiest Now

It is the special point of our present study that the Blood is essential to our entrance into the Holiest now. In the old Tabernacle and Temple, there was a Veil that barred access into the holiest, except by one man, on one day in each year. When he, the High Priest, entered, he took in with him the Blood of the sacrifice that he had offered as God appointed. When Christ died, that actual Veil was split down from the top, as we learn from Matthew 27:51, as the sign and signal that His Body— "His flesh," as our passage in Hebrews 10:20 calls it— was "cleft for me." By that rending, the way in was thrown open to all believers. Our Great High Priest has gone in first to ensure our acceptance "with His own Blood" (Hebrews 9:12). On the ground of that Precious Blood of atonement for sin we dare to enter. Yea, we are invited to enter even "with boldness."

This study has been of a rather more doctrinal nature than usual. But it will probably do us no harm on that account! Here is another of our Prayer Secrets. Like its companions, it is one that will make a deep impression on our time of fellowship with the Holy One. When we come into the Holy Presence to pray, let us pause for a moment on the Threshold to ponder over this, that it is only "by the Blood of Jesus" that we can venture further in. Let us also wonder at this, that on the ground of the same Precious Blood, we have (and none can gainsay us) unchallenged entry!

The 20th verse of our chapter calls this "a new and living way," and it is very interesting to note that the "new" is really "newly slain." The word is used nowhere else in Scripture, and is evidently intended to convey the idea, not that the Sacrifice ever needs to be freshly reoffered, as some teach, but that the One Sacrifice once offered remains ever fresh in saving efficacy. It is as if He died but yesterday, as if His Precious Blood were shed for us this morning. This is what a very "advanced" Anglican, "Father" Stanton, meant when he said, "Calvary has no date!" Throughout the eternity of the past—for the Lamb was "slain from the foundation of the world" (Revelation 13:8; 1 Peter 1:19–20); throughout the eternity of the future—for He is recognized in Heaven as "a Lamb as it had been slain" (Revelation 5:6); throughout the intervening stretch of time—He is ever "the same yesterday, and today and forever" (Hebrews 13:8), always "newly–slain," as well as "ever–living" (Hebrews 7:25). So, as we pass the Threshold into the place of prayer, by the way of the Precious Blood, may we be ever freshly conscious of its amazing grace, and ever freshly grateful for its glorious efficacy—today, as ever!

4

The Atmosphere

"The throne of grace"—Hebrews 4:16

When, by Invitation, we enter the Presence, across the Threshold of the Blood, we ask what will be the Atmosphere of the place to which we come. The text conveys the sense of that atmosphere very clearly. It tells us that, whatever else it is, the place where we have come to pray is a "throne of grace." That fact does three things that are of very great importance to our prayer life.

It Puts Us In Our Right Place

A Sense of Our Smallness

We wonder, almost instinctively, what we ordinary folks are doing in the place of a Throne, and that, indeed, the Throne of the Universe. We know at once our littleness, and anything that teaches us that is good. An old veteran in God's service told some young Christian workers who were gathered about him, "You can easily become too big for God to use you, but you can never become too little." How true. Nowhere more true is that than in the sphere of service and of prayer. To learn true humility is to learn one of the greatest of the Prayer Secrets.

A Sense of Our Sinfulness

Our text also gives us a sense of our sinfulness. It is a "throne of grace," and indeed, if it where any other kind of throne, we could not dare to approach. The mere fact of its character throws up the sinful nature of our own character, as surely as a fall of snow would throw up the yellow dinginess of the newly–washed linen that, till then, had seemed so white and clean. There is no sort of doubt that a real apprehension of our phrase will most certainly put us in our right place.

It Shows Him in His True Light

What sort of Person is He Who sits upon the Throne? Never let us forget that there are two sides to His character which seem mutually contradictory, but are, in fact, possessed and held in perfect poise and balance. They are goodness and severity, love and justice. To emphasize the one side to the exclusion of, or at the expense of, the other is always to court disaster.

There have been whole epochs of Christian history in which the severity and justice of God have been so completely taught that the softer, and sweeter, and gentler aspects have been almost ousted from men's thoughts. Religion has seemed hard, and harsh, and cold. That, one imagines, is not our danger today. We have, in our turn, so dwelt upon the love of God that His sterner sides are almost forgotten. The truth is, of course, that both aspects are true, and that our wisdom lies in holding them in Scriptural relation. Only so can we see Him in His true light, which is what our text helps us to do.

An Image of Majesty

We see a Person of majesty. He is on a throne. Think what a deep impression was made upon the young prophet when, in Isaiah 6:1, he "saw the Lord . . . sitting upon a throne." There will be no frivolity, and no undue familiarity about our time of prayer when we realize this aspect of the case.

An Image of Mercy

He occupies a throne indeed, but a throne of grace. His seat is a mercy seat. His majesty will not deter us, will not drive us from Him in confusion and despair, for His mercy bids us come and even "come boldly." Such is the Atmosphere that prevails in the audience chamber—composed of these two seemingly opposite qualities.

Need In Its Real Proportions

Does Our Need Seem Big To Us?

We are constrained to ask, does our need seem big to us? Then make quite sure that God knows how big it looks to our eyes, and He will treat it accordingly. He will never belittle it, and however trivial it may be in reality, He will not laugh at it, or at us. He never forgets how large it looms to us.

Does Our Need Seem As Big As

The Throne of Grace?

We ask further, does our need seem as big as the throne of grace? Do we not there, and there only, see it in its real proportions? Do you remember how Paul, inspired by the Holy Spirit, deals in Philippians 4:19 with "your need"? Taken out of its context, how enormous it seems. Viewed thus in isolation, it appears at times almost beyond meeting. Yet, see how he hangs this picture. On the one side he places this other one, "My God"—what vast conceptions it conjures up to faith's vision: the unmeasured, and forever immeasurable ability of the Triune God. On the further side, we find this picture, "His riches"—what depths, and what details are in it! What an impression we get of unplumbed inexhaustibility. It is in between these two amazing canvases that "your need" is shown—a picture, big enough in itself, but in comparison, dwarfed to its real proportions. So does need of every kind shrink when brought up to "the throne of grace."

Prayer In Its Proper Character

The verse in Hebrews from which our little text is taken tells us that we come to prayer for a twofold purpose—to "obtain mercy," and to "find . . . help." The juxtaposition of those two phrases shows, in no uncertain way, the nature of the occupation upon which we are there employed.

Not An Application

It is not an application, merely as if by some transaction between equals, and by the exercise of right, we had only to apply for help to secure it automatically. This is not true prayer's character.

But A Supplication

It is a supplication, as by one who must first "obtain mercy" before he can hope to "find . . . help." He approaches, and he asks, not on the ground of his own deserving, but on that of Divine "grace." If that be his attitude, he may come expectantly.

Thus, the "place where prayer is wont to be made" has an Atmosphere all its own. It is because it aids in the creation of such a feeling that our text is so helpful a Prayer Secret.

5

The Address

"When ye pray, say, 'Our Father' "
Luke 11:2

In the previous chapter we were bidden to recognize and realize the Sovereignty of the One to Whom we come in prayer. Yet, now we learn to our undying amazement that we are to address Him as "our Father." I expect that the little princesses of Buckingham Palace, while never allowed to forget that His Majesty is King, are yet permitted to address him as "Father." Such is the situation of God's children when they desire to speak to Him. The implications of this truth are so tremendous as to make it another of our Prayer Secrets.

The Introduction Into the Family

Only those who enjoy that privileged position are entitled to use this "familiar" address.

The Universal Fatherhood of God

The universal Fatherhood of God is a doctrine widely held in these days, yet only in a material and philosophical sense can He be called "The Father of the Universe."

The Individual Fatherhood of God

The individual Fatherhood of God, in the spiritual and eternal sense, is a truth applicable to none except true believers. The Holy Spirit inspired John to write that "as many as received Him, to them gave He the power [right, privilege, authority] to become the sons of God" (John 1:12). Paul writes, "ye are all [that is, all you Christians, for it is to such that the Epistles were written, and to such only that they apply] the children of God by faith in Christ Jesus" (Galatians 3:26). New birth in the family of God by the regenerating operation of the Holy Spirit takes place at the very moment when receiving faith in the Saviour is exercised by the individual. At that instant, the person concerned is gloriously, eternally, and miraculously introduced into the family of "our Father." Oh, wondrous grace and love of God!

The Instruction of the Son

By His Example

Christ teaches us by His example, for it was always His way to use the filial address. On seven occasions we are told the actual words that He used in prayer—Matthew 11:25; 26:39, 42; Luke 23:34, 46; John 12: 28; 17:1. Each time it is as "Father" that He addresses the Most High. How much we could learn, not only in this, but also in the other, particularly if we would watch the Master at prayer. That the Divine Son should so be so frequently praying, that He should find such solace and such strength therein, is a striking lesson in itself.

By His Express Injunction

In addition to His example, He guides us by His express injunction. He directs that we are to begin our prayers as He did. Let us be clear that it cannot be wrong to pray to Jesus Himself, for He is God. Neither can it be wrong to pray to the Holy Spirit, for He is God. But the Lord is here instructing us in what is to be the normal procedure. Prayer is usually to be thought of as being *to* the Father, *by* the Spirit, ***through*** the Son. The Son knows how the sons should approach the throne. He tells us that our ordinary habit should be to say "Our Father." What a great effect this will produce upon our heart, and upon our prayer life, when we really grasp it.

The Implication of the Relationship

The Father's Love Wants the

Best for His Children

The Father's love desires the best for His own. That is true upon the merely human plane, and when the love is God's love, it is intensified manifold. Whatever is good for us, He wants us to have. It stands written that "no good thing will He withhold from them that walk upright" (Psalm 84:11). When, therefore, we come to Him with our request, we may rest assured that, if it be for our highest welfare, He is no less anxious than we that it should be granted us.

The Father's Wisdom Knows the
Best for His Children

In the human sphere, love is not always wise. The fond parent may err exceedingly as to what is best for the beloved child. This is a problem that can never arise in the higher relationship, for His love never outruns His wisdom. So exactly do the two qualities correspond in Him, that any refusal we may have is a sure indication that the thing we asked for is not for our good, and therefore His loving "No" may be accepted trustingly and cheerfully.

The Father's Power Does the
Best for His Children

Over and over again in the human family, the thing which the parent wants the child to have, and which is known to be good and wise is not given, because it is not within the ability of the parent to grant it. How different it is in God's case. What His love dictates and His wisdom approves, His power can supply!

Such are some of the precious things that lie implicit in the Fatherhood of God toward us. Our prayers are bound to be colored by such thoughts if they are properly understood. We never can be thankful enough that the Master directed us, "When ye pray, say, 'Our Father,'" seeing that so much is wrapped up in the fact that we are permitted to speak upon the ground of such a relationship. Truly, we say again, a wondrous Prayer Secret is here.

The use of that word "Our" in the address stresses for us the fact that we are not lone individuals, but members of a family. It also underlines that we are not the sole member of the family. This is one of the reasons why, in dealing with prayer, the Master has emphasized so often the necessity for that harmony, which we consider in a later study.

In the life of a well-regulated earthly family, the father will not listen to the requests of anyone of his children who is squabbling with his brothers and sisters—no favors for the quarrelsome would be his rule. In the higher, more serious realm, that same rule holds—"first be reconciled" is His direction. How important then, and how powerful, that we may each individually, or all together, come with our requests to "Our Father," knowing how thoroughly He understands His children, and each child, and knowing how thoroughly He can satisfy them when they come. Yes, to learn to address Him properly is one of the big Secrets.

6

The Key

"In My Name"—John 15:16

The Name is not just a kind of lucky charm which, if tacked on to the end of a prayer, will secure the desired benefit. Rather, it is a wonderful key which, if properly used, will unlock the King's treasure, and open to us the Father's resources. What a grand Secret of successful prayer it therefore becomes.

On the last night that our Lord spent with His disciples in the flesh, He had with them a last precious and solemn talk. It is recorded in John 14—16. One of the subjects that He discussed (and He discussed only those things that were of vital significance and importance), was this matter of prayer. One of the striking things about His treatment of it is the fact that, within the comparatively small compass of those three chapters, He used that phrase "In My Name" no less than seven times.

Another striking thing is the fact that such amazing promises are attached to prayer in His Name—promises, indeed, which embrace "whatsoever," and "anything," that His disciples ask. These two facts make it plain that we are fully justified in calling this Secret "the Key," and make it also supremely important that we should try to understand the nature of the key. With diffidence, then, I offer the suggestion that prayer in the Name means at least three things.

The Name Is the
Introduction of Prayer

Our Name Unworthy

Let it be at once acknowledged that in the Courts of Heaven our name stands for unworthiness. To present our petition in our name would be to court refusal and disappointment. But, what if we are introduced by Another?

His Name Supreme

Let it ever be remembered that in Heaven's Court One Name stands supreme. It is "a Name which is above every name" (Philippians 2:9). There is a phrase with which we generally finish our prayers: "through Jesus Christ our Lord," and which all too often we use hurriedly, formally, and almost unthinkingly. But what if, in reality, it should be rather the most important part of the prayer? Its meaning is that our petition is presented through Him. Without the introduction we should get no hearing in the royal Audience Chamber. His Name is sufficient to secure acceptance of our person, and attention to our petition. That is part of what it means to pray "In My Name."

The Name Is the Signature of Prayer

We Are Permitted to Use His Name

The remarkable thing is that we are allowed to use His Name. "Ask anything in My Name, I will do it," says the Master in John 14:14. But that sounds uncommonly like a duly signed blank check. It is good for "anything" (up to the limit of the need), and it is acceptably guaranteed by the Name which is always honored in the Celestial Bank. To present the check, then, bearing His Name—that is to offer prayer "in My Name"—is as if it were not merely we, but He, making the request. Is it not a truly remarkable thing that we are encouraged thus to use His signature?

We Are to be Careful Not to Misuse His Name

At the same time, we are to be careful not to misuse it. We must see to it that we ask nothing that He could not put His Name to. That brings me to the last thing I want to say with regard to this particular aspect of prayer.

The Name Is the Character of Prayer

All our prayers are to be in accord with His Name, with His nature, with His known character, if they are to be granted.

An Acquaintance With Him

To this end there must be an acquaintance with Him, a knowledge of His mind. "We have the mind of Christ," says Paul in 1 Corinthians 2:16—just as an ambassador may be said to have the mind of his sovereign. It comes only from personal touch. So, by a close study of His Word, and by a close walk with Him in daily trust and obedience, we shall come to possess His mind, and know instinctively what He would think about matters, and thus be able to avoid asking anything that would be out of tune with His character and His purpose. Such a man as George Müller was able to ask so successfully because he had come to know Christ so well. But, knowledge by itself is not sufficient.

A Harmony With Him

There must also be harmony with Him. There can be no effective use of His Name if our wills are not adjusted to His will, if our desires are at variance with His desires, if our lives are at cross–purposes with Him.

A Union With Him

Indeed, to get to the bottom of this business, there must be a union with Him. This blessed intimacy of relationship between the Lord and His own is indicated by many illustrations in the Scriptures. We are the branches in the Vine (John 15:5); we are limbs in the Body (1 Corinthians 12:27); we are members of the Family (1 John 3:1); we are the bride of Christ (Ephesians 5:25).

When a man marries a girl, she ceases to use her own name and begins to use his. If she had been poor before, what a difference his name will now make. She can make requests in his name that would never have been heeded in her own. So does the heavenly Bridegroom bestow upon us His Name, and entrust it to our care and use. If we know Him, and are in harmony with Him, and are even united to Him, we can so effectively use His Name that when we pray a prayer, it is as if He prayed it. That is why the "whatsoever" promises are attached to it. The character of the Name shapes the character of the prayer.

To pray, then, in His Name, means to pray in such a way that the petition is in complete harmony with the whole nature of Christ. It is as if ours would be, both in word and in spirit, the very prayer He would pray if He were in our circumstances—"if He stood in my shoes," as Mr. B.C. Plowright put it. That is not easily come by. It demands a life of such obedience that it may truly be said that we "abide" in Him. It calls for a growth of such acquaintance of His Word that it may indeed be said that His "words" abide in us (John 15:7). Then, because the petition would thus be in His Name, "it shall be done."

7

The Guarantee

"Anything according to His will"
1 John 5:14

There is no manner of doubt that we are given a specific guarantee in God's Word that prayer shall be answered, and that guarantee is His will. Within the compass of that will He has pledged Himself to grant the petitions we desire. Such a guarantee is a great incentive and secret of prayer.

The Permit

In His will there lies the permit. It is not only that we are allowed, in general, to come to Him in prayer. That truth has been taught us over and over again already in our study of these Secrets. We have got a little further along now.

Permits Our Confidence

His will permits our confidence. "We ask," indeed, in that spirit, as this passage directs us. We approach the throne, not in a fearful or doubtful attitude, but with "boldness."

Permits Our Reliance

Moreover, His will permits our reliance. "We have," indeed, such assurance of the prayer's fulfillment that the thing is already as good as ours.

The Limit

Let it be remembered that His will is the limit. However wide the promise to prayer may seem to be with its "whatsoever," it must ever be borne in mind that the limit of His will is always implied. That is the only limit— "anything according to His will" is specifically guaranteed!

His Will Not an Unknown

His will is not to be thought of as an unknown quantity, as if we could not be sure what it really was, and could only hope that what we ask for proves to be within its range. Those who have such a conception are content with a merely negative result. If they do not get what they ask for, they assume that the thing was not in accordance with His will and leave it at that. Yet, surely the passage from which we have taken our text does not mean us to be satisfied with such an attitude. It tells us that His will is to beget "confidence" in our praying. But what confidence can we secure from such a conception as we have outlined? Some different idea is quite evidently intended.

His Will a Well–Known Guide

His will is to be sought for as a well–known guide, as if we were to be so certain that the petition was His wish that we were confident that we should obtain it. Is there any secret whereby we can arrive at such a practical knowledge of His will?

You see at once the tremendous importance of this point. First, His Word gives us the broad principles of God's will, and that with such clarity that we can, as a rule, make day–by–day application of it to particular needs and situations. But this means a constant study of the Word under the Holy Spirit's guidance. The more we come to know His Word, the more we shall (as it were, instinctively) know His will, and be thus guided, among other things, in our prayer life. We shall learn increasingly to avoid asking for what the Holy Scriptures have taught us to discern as not in accordance with His will. The second thing is that the surest and quickest way of coming to know the likely wishes and will of people is to go and live with them. With all reverence, we say that it is possible for us to live so close to the Lord that we may come to recognize (again, as it were, instinctively) what His will would probably be on any matter. Living with Him, abiding in Him, is (to put it into everyday, matter-of–fact language), obeying Him. Abiding simply means obeying. As we obey, we abide, and so come to know His mind, His will.

Let us put these two things we have spoken of in Scriptural words—"If ye abide in Me, and My words abide in you, ye shall ask what ye will, and it shall be done unto you" (John 15:7). How so? Because those two things bring us to know God's will and to ask only within that Divinely imposed limit. "What ye will" being "according to His will," we can indeed ask with confidence.

The Summit

The Depths

Another thought is that His will is the summit. We sometimes speak of the will of God as if it were the depths. If we must sing about it, we make a dirge of it. We talk as if it were something to be endured. We brace ourselves to be resigned. Have we ever thought what a travesty all this is of God's purposes, what a slander and insult it is of His love?

The Heights

The exact opposite is the truth. His will is the heights. "Thou sweet beloved will of God," as the old hymn writer has it. Dr. S.D. Gordon once said that "the purpose of prayer is to get God's will done." What a flood of light that sentence throws upon the whole matter! The summit of all prayer is, "Thy will be done." Truly, "His will" must be included among the greatest of our Prayer Secrets, for it is the God–given guarantee of all answered prayer.

You will likely be familiar with the working of a combination lock, and you know that when the appropriate spots on the various discs coincide, the lock can be turned and access gained to the safe or the house. Somewhat the same it is in the case of prayer, that when our will is brought to the place where it coincides with His will, the combination is secured which ensures that the key of prayer can successfully turn the lock of His storehouse and obtain the answer to our need. When "my will" says "Thy will," we may reckon upon the best of all answers to our prayers—for His will is synonymous with His best. As a hymn writer put it, "He gives the very best to those who leave the choice to Him."

If we are to "ask anything according to His will," that He may hear us, how important it is that we should possess "the knowledge of His will" (Colossians 1:9), as Paul prays for his friends. Such knowledge comes only from a diligent study of His Word and an obedient walk in His way. May this be ours!

8

The Instructor

"The Spirit also helpeth our infirmities"
Romans 8:26

There is much that we need to learn about the subject and practice of prayer. There is One Who is willing to teach us. The Holy Spirit is only too ready to instruct us in this noblest of all employments. This is by no means the least of the things that He does for the believer, and His connection with our prayer life is one of the biggest of our Prayer Secrets. Let us, then, think about four ways in which He helps our infirmities.

He Prepares Us

We never forget that prayer is audience with the King, and we rejoice to know that He has Himself invited us to that audience and has arranged everything to secure our admittance and to ensure our welcome.

Presumption

We do well to remember that we must not rush into the Presence just as we like. There is a dress, a deportment becoming to a royal audience at Buckingham Palace, and no one who deliberately neglected such requirements would be received. Are we to suppose that access to the Divine Presence is, in contrast to this, a merely slipshod affair, requiring no thought and no preparation of the heart, and making no demands upon our readiness of spirit?

Preparation

On the contrary, we are to take care that we are prepared for the Presence. We should be "clothed with humility," and we are to approach "in the beauty of holiness." Whenever we come to intercede at the Throne, let us spend a preliminary period of silence in seeking adjustment of heart and preparedness of spirit. This will be no wasted time. Rather, it will set its mark upon the whole of the subsequent ministry of prayer. The Blessed Holy Spirit is the One Who can do this for us.

He Guides Our Initial Approach

Speaking For God

He will guide our first steps. This is true of our first speaking for God. It not infrequently happens that new converts are held back from confessing Christ because of shyness or nervousness. They don't know what to say, or they fear that they would only break down and make fools of themselves. Yet, all the while, the Holy Spirit is ready to help them over their first steps in testimony. Do you remember Acts 2:4—"They were all filled with the Holy Ghost and began to speak . . . ." Never mind the "other tongues" of that verse. It is your own tongue which is your trouble, and He will guide you there.

But that is not our subject just now.

Speaking To God

Our present concern is that this thing is true of our first speaking to God. That is a lovely thought that we have in Galatians 4:6, "Because ye are sons, God hath sent forth the Spirit of His Son into your hearts, crying, Abba." It is the very first lisping of the "babe in Christ," and the Holy Spirit helps us thus begin speaking to our Father in Heaven. If you say that word "Abba" carefully, you will notice that it does not need any teeth to make the sounds. A little thing could learn to say the word before it gets its teeth. So can the newest infant in the spiritual life be taught by the Holy Spirit the "ABC's" of prayer.

He Guides Subsequent Desires

Desires Expressed

He will give our subsequent desires. It is the experience of us all that generally, those desires are expressed in definite petitions. Nowhere is our infirmity more apparent than in our deep need to be taught how to ask for the right things, "for we know not what we should pray for as we ought." One of the blessed results of being "filled with the Holy Ghost" is that we may ask Him to see that our "intercession" is, as verse 27 of our passage says, "according to the will of God," and that our specific desires may thus, as we have seen before, look confidently for fulfillment.

Desires Inexpressible

Occasionally, those desires are too deep to be expressed in words, and even then the inarticulate longings of our hearts may truly be the motions of the Holy Spirit Himself interceding for us with the "groanings that cannot be uttered," to which verse 26 refers. God Who knows the heart understands when these unexpressed yearnings are the implantings of the Spirit, when they are the embodiment of "the mind of the Spirit."

Do you remember how, in Genesis 21:17, it says that God "heard the voice of the lad"? It was not in his words, for in the distress of his circumstances he probably did not say any words. But God understood and answered his unspoken desires. A mother hears her little one cry, and in some mysterious way, knows exactly what the child is saying, though no word is spoken! God, too, understands such language, and recognizes when the desire so conveyed is the result of the Spirit's working within us. He knows when it is His intercession within us "with groanings that cannot be uttered." Jude 20 speaks of "praying in the Holy Ghost." Perhaps these thoughts suggest that praying in Him means having Him pray in us. What a mighty Prayer Secret we have been touching on!

He Will Get Glory for Christ

Through the Whole Life

The Holy Spirit will get glory for Jesus. It is that for which He is always working. That is His great passion—

"He shall glorify Me" (John 16:14). Through the believer's whole life He will secure that, if the believer is completely surrendered and daily filled.

Through the Prayer Life

Our present point is that He will secure glory for Christ through the believer's prayer life, if we seek to learn how to pray triumphantly. All our Prayer Secrets will help us to that end, and not least, this secret of implicit trust and obedience to our Divine Instructor in the school of prayer. "Our infirmities," of which Romans 8:26 speaks, are such that we can never, of ourselves, glorify the Lord Jesus. Nowhere is this so apparent as in our prayer life. "We know not what we should pray for as we ought," the verse says. That means that, of ourselves, we fail first as to the What, and then as to the How. We said all this earlier. We only repeat it now in order to emphasize and underline the great truth that the Holy Spirit both can and will meet us in our "infirmities," and so take charge of our prayer life as to turn it into a mighty instrument for the Master's Glory.

9

The Reservoir of God's Resources

"According to His riches"
Philippians 4:19

It is sometimes helpful to think about the amazing reservoir from which God is able to supply whatever is necessary for the answering of our prayers. Romans 2:4 speaks of it as "the riches of His goodness," and in Ephesians 1:7 it is "the riches of His grace," while Ephesians 3:6 has "the riches of His glory." What a mighty reservoir are those riches!

How Great the Supply

Riches Beyond Measure

How large is the supply. It must be recognized that no one can count His riches. Paul gives up trying to reckon the sum, and simply says, "O the depth . . ." (Romans 11:33).

Riches Beyond Measuring

Of course, no one need count His riches. It is enough

to know that they are more than adequate to cover "all your need," as the context of our opening phrase teaches us. And Paul was not talking about something that he did not understand. He was not merely repeating what other people said. There was many an occasion in his own experience when he had reason to thank God for the "boundless stores of grace." You recall, for instance, that time when he received his Master's definite assurance, "My grace is sufficient for thee" (2 Corinthians 12:9). So we begin to grasp that, however great the size of our need, however large the scope of our prayer, the supply is always greater than the demand. We shall never find our God at a loss for the means to satisfy our real requirement. That is something worth remembering as we come to pray.

How Varied the Supply

The Variety of the Requests

There is no need to stress the variety of the requests that we must make of Him—they are as different as our personalities, as different as our circumstances, as different as our temptations.

The Variety of the Resources

But all this is matched by the variety of the resources that He has at His disposal. There is a very interesting Greek word used twice in the New Testament, and each time by Peter. It is translated "manifold." In 1 Peter 1:6, we have "manifold temptations"—testings, trials. Then in 1 Peter 4:10, we have "manifold grace"—different kinds of grace. Let your left hand represent the former—thumb and fingers, each different from the other, standing for the manifold needs. Let your right hand represent the other side of the matter—thumb and fingers meeting those of the left, and exactly corresponding. So do His resources not only cover, but also coincide with your requests. It is good to know that when, as in Hebrews 4:16, we "come boldly unto the throne . . that we may . . . find grace," we may get exactly the sort of grace that will help the sort of need that drove us to make our petition.

How Secure the Supply

The Ravages of Earth Cannot Tarnish It

How secure is the supply. It is so safe that the circumstances of earth cannot tarnish it, for it is "in glory," that place "where neither moth nor rust doth corrupt," as the Master tells us in Matthew 6:20.

The Devices of Men Cannot Diminish It

It is so safe that the machinations of men cannot diminish it, for it is "in Christ Jesus," that strong Hiding place "where thieves do not break through nor steal."

Suppose we had to depend upon a source of help that might dry up! No, on second thought, why suppose any such thing, for the fact is that our Supply will never even diminish, let alone disappear. It is there, all there, always there.

How Lavish the Supply

Not Out Of

How lavish is the supply. The glory of this truth has been for many folks obscured by a false quotation, the phrase being given as "out of His riches." It is, of course, the case that He does assist us out of His riches, as a wealthy man like Lord Nuffield would do if he gave a poor beggar a shilling. That miserable pittance would come of the rich man's very great resources, and "out of " carries no further implication than that.

But According To

The true quotation is "according to," and that implies something very different. Lord Nuffield's behavior to his beggar will now be on a wholly more beneficent plane. Instead of a mere shilling, he will offer something more consonant with his own wealth. Perhaps he will set him up in business, and open a bank account for him. Nothing would be too little for "out of "; nothing would be too much for "according to"!

God is ever desirous of dealing abundantly with His beggars. Have we not often found that out in our own personal experience? "Enough and to spare" (Luke 15:17) is not only an account of what is laid up in the Father's house, but is also the measure of the way the Father loves to give—up to the limit of our need, and a bit more.

All this is a great encouragement to those who pray. Therefore, I think I am justified in including the thought of the Reservoir in the list of our Prayer Secrets. Truly, "none can ever ask too much." There is a word in Ephesians 2:4 which says that "God . . . is rich," and that wealth embraces every commodity and every currency. This is the One with Whom we have to do, a God of infinite resources, dispensed by infinite love. Here is a Bank that never breaks. No demand made upon it will find it wanting or unready, for "it" is He. Come then, ye sinners and ye saints. Here is plenty. Here is grace abounding!

10

The Scope

*"In everything by prayer . . . supplication
. . . requests"—Philippians 4:6*

The compass of prayer embraces every aspect and activity of life: the big things as well as the little things, the little things no less than the big things—"everything"! Indeed, if there is anything in our lives that cannot be prayed about, we may be quite sure that that thing has no business being there at all.

How comforting it is to know that, as this passage teaches us, we need be anxious about nothing, if only we will make everything the subject of prayer. The three words used here in our verse for our petitioning the throne of grace are interesting. It is not easy to draw a line of clear distinction between them, but perhaps we may venture to differentiate somewhat.

Prayer In General

Prayer as a Habit

Prayer in general seems to be the wide embrace of the first word, "prayer." It suggests prayer as a habit, as much so as getting into bed and getting out of bed. The first thing in the morning and the last thing at night, it is our regular custom, almost our routine, to pray. The cycle of our daily prayers will include "everything."

Prayer as a Law

We make prayer our rule of life, both to seek God's blessing on "everything"—spiritual or material, secular or sacred—and to seek God's guidance in "everything," so that we may know and do His will all along the way. But, notice the scope of this. It is Everything!

Prayer in Particular

Prayer in particular appears to be the significance of our second word, "supplication." It is not the whole thought of prayer that is now in mind, but the petition about some specific matter.

In the Universal Sphere

It may be in the universal sphere, for prayer is so wide in its scope as to be able to take the whole world in its grasp. The Christian is placed in the world, and he must, therefore, seek by all means within his power to influence that world for good and for God. One of the most powerful means at his disposal is this use of prayer. He may effect some very definite impression upon the worldwide cause of God, or in the solution of international problems.

Have you ever thought of using your newspaper as a Prayer Book? Try it one day, and see how God will lead you out in prayer. I warn you that you will need to set aside a long time for the purpose, but how real it will all be, and how fruitful! When God says "everything," He means nothing less, and "everything" includes the gigantic affairs of a universe.

In the National Sphere

Prayer is so practical in its scope as to reach out to and touch the life of a nation. The leaders of a nation have a claim upon our prayers, for we are exhorted to intercede "for kings and for all that are in authority" (1 Timothy 2:1-2). The condition of the nation makes an urgent call for prayer-warriors, seeing that the enemy of souls is so busy among us, and that he has proved so successful in his propaganda and in his projects. The peril of the people, and therefore, the need of the people is not primarily material, but spiritual. It is in that sphere that the weapon of prayer is conspicuously, so preeminently powerful. In any case, it would be wrong to omit our country from our prayers when the Lord said, "Everything," wouldn't it?

In the Personal Sphere

Prayer is so intimate in its scope that it embraces our individual needs and longings. Once again let it be emphasized that in this sphere also there is no limit to the range of prayer interest. "Everything" may properly be included. "O what peace we often forfeit, O what needless pain we bear, All because we do not carry 'Everything' to God in prayer."

Prayer in Detail

Prayer in detail is the point of that last word, "requests." First, there is the general attitude of prayer. Next, there is the particular subject of prayer. And now, we have the special points of detail concerning that subject.

Dividing Prayer Into Details

We are encouraged thus to break up our prayer into details. Take such a passage as Luke 11:9–12. We have first the general, "ask," in verse 9. We have next the particular, "ask bread," in verse 11. We may pray concerning our food. Then, it is broken up into detail: "bread . . . fish . . . egg," in verses 11–12.

Prayer About the Ordinary

We may presume, therefore, to deal in our prayer with details. The Lord is interested in the odd sparrow thrown in (compare Luke 12:6 with Matthew 10:29). The Lord is concerned for "the very hairs of your head" (Matthew 10:30). Observe, please, that it is not merely "hair" in general, but "hairs" in detail. He is always glad that we should speak with Him about the ordinary items of daily life, the little things of personal need.

A little boy who wrote to me some years ago was assuredly acting within his Christian rights when he was able to tell me, "I pray to Jesus now, and I get nine sums right out of ten." The Master was interested in His child's sums, just as He is interested in the details of your life.

We said earlier that "Everything" includes the big things. Let us learn now that it also includes the little things. To grasp both of these truths is to understand one of the big Prayer Secrets given us in the Word.

This, then, is the Scope of our prayer–warrant—"Everything" in general, in particular, and in detail. A warrant so comprehensive, so extensive, and so intensive makes of prayer a tremendously important thing. There are some husbands and wives whose happy boast is that they tell each other everything, and talk over everything together. So it is in the ideal relationship between the believer and his Lord. To refer everything to Him should become "second nature" to us. When that widest possible scope of prayerfulness becomes the experience of our daily habit, then "the peace of God, which passeth all understanding shall keep your hearts and minds through Christ Jesus." These words are Paul's testimony out from the midst of his prison, not out of an easygoing comfort! That is why the peace is beyond understanding. But thank God, it is not beyond experiencing.

11

The Lookout

"Watch and pray"—Matthew 26:41

The vessel sailing through danger–infested waters needs to maintain a constant "lookout." And so does the ship of prayer. No one is a firmer believer in the power of prayer than the devil, not that he practices it, but he suffers from it. The hymn writer was justified in saying, "Satan trembles when he sees the weakest saint upon his knees." That is why the evil one is so assiduous in trying to disturb the prayer life of believers. It is one of the reasons why it is so important to watch as well as to pray. What, then, is the relationship between prayerfulness and watchfulness?

Watch Before You Pray

When we propose to pray, or when we go to pray, the devil will do his utmost either to prevent it or to spoil it. Therefore, it is so highly important to be on our guard against him.

A Quiet Mind

It is infinitely desirable that we should go to our prayer with a quiet mind. To rush in thoughtlessly, heedlessly, breathlessly is to hamper and hinder the whole interview. Nowhere is it more necessary than here to "study to be quiet" (1 Thessalonians 4:11). We must beware lest the enemy, by some trick or turn of our circumstances, throw us into a turmoil.

A Right Spirit

We must also have a right spirit, seeking not anything else than the will of God. Here again the adversary will be on the alert to trip us up if he can. Be on the lookout, then, before you go to your work of intercession.

Watch While You Pray

The Sleepy Body

Even at the moment when we are engaged upon this holy business, there are snares for the unwary. It was this trouble which elicited our text from the Master. His three intimates had been sadly overcome by slumber in the garden of Gethsemane, when He had craved their sympathetic companionship in prayerful vigilance.

Which of us has not at some time or other had woeful experience of this hindrance to prayer? Indeed, we have known of some who have given up the practice of the morning's quiet time because they simply could not keep awake! What is to be said of such folks? Two words, I think, and they are "Physical Jerks." Does this seem a strange thing to include in a treatise on Prayer Secrets? You must decide for yourself, but I will give it to you as my own experience that a few physical exercises, by toning up the muscles and setting the blood flowing, have often banished sleepiness from the frame and thus prepared the way for prayer. Perhaps we should have included this in the previous section on Watching before you pray as "an alert body." If this is one of your troubles, try this commonplace secret.

The Wandering Thought

Next we would consider the wandering thought. This is where so many would–be intercessors fail so unhappily. How many have spoken with distress and even with shame of their defeat in this way. We must try to say something about this very common and distressing phenomenon. I really think there is no need to discuss here either the nature or the source of these thoughts. It will be more profitable if we devote our small space to the secret of deliverance from their bondage.

Let me venture to say that I do not believe there is any easy way to victory. These unruly thoughts must be brought under Christ's sway after the manner of 2 Corinthians 10:5—"bringing into captivity every thought to the obedience of Christ." As each rebel thought or imagination appears, you must instantly arrest it in the Name of the King. The more this is practiced, the more quickly and the more completely you will have control of the situation. Perseverance and patience will bring their own reward.

The Intruding Self

We must also be watchful against the force of self. "How many subtle forms it takes, of seeming verity."

You know as well as I do the ways in which self enters and spoils. Even Elijah, that great man of prayer, finds the answer temporarily held up because a little bit of self creeps into his motive—"let it be known this day that . . . I am Thy servant, and that I have done all these things at Thy word" (1 Kings 18:36). At the momentary delay he pursues his prayer more passionately. Finally, upon the complete elimination of self, the answer came— "Then!"

The Lurking Foe

Even while we pray we must be prepared for the lurking foe. He doesn't want you to pray, and if you persist, he doesn't want you to pray effectually. Therefore, you have to reckon upon his opposition. How needful it is, at such a time, to watch as well as pray.

Watch After You Pray

If you are a golfer you will know how important to your strokes is the "follow through"—a clean hit, a hard hit, a straight hit depend so much upon what you do with your club immediately after impact with the ball. You must learn to watch after you play, and, after you pray!

The Answer

The effectiveness of prayer is sometimes lost through a weak "after watching." Be keenly on the lookout for the answers to your prayers, and learn to recognize them even if they do not come in the way you expect.

The Opportunity

God will often answer by opening the way for you to answer your own prayer. If you ask for someone's conversion or blessing, He may give you the chance to be His instrument or agent. Be quick to see and seize any such opportunity after prayer. That sensible saint Hugh Redwood has put it thus, "We dare not pray to God in another's behalf unless we are ready, and even eager, to be used to the limit in His response."

The Rest

When you rise from your knees, leave the burden at God's feet. Let Him see that, having prayed, you really do trust Him, and can be quite at rest about it all. Such a resting faith is ever a God–honoring thing. That makes for effective praying. So, whichever way you look at it, watching is one of the big Prayer Secrets.

12

The Word

"Take . . . the Word of God: praying"
Ephesians 6:17–18

When we go praying, it is of immense importance that we should take the Word with us, for there is a very intimate connection between effectual prayer and the devotional reading of Holy Scripture. We are not thinking just now about the more prolonged and more detailed and more solid study of the Bible. That also is a matter vital to spiritual well–being. But our concern at the moment is with the simpler method. Several things are to be said about it.

It Begets Fellowship

We Speak With Him

Our quiet time with God is not meant to be a monologue, but a dialogue. It is true that we speak with Him. That is one of the simplest conceptions of prayer. Of course, some people only speak to the ceiling, and others do not even get as far as that. "The Pharisee stood and prayed thus with himself" (Luke 18:11). But when we are sincere and real, and not merely formal, God is so marvelously gracious that He actually does allow us to speak with Him.

He Speaks With Us

It is also true that He speaks with us. His normal means of communication is the Word. So, we "take . . . the Word of God" when we are "praying." It is essential that this kind of reading of the Scriptures shall be unhurried, so it is probably wise to confine ourselves to a small portion, doubtless in some regular course of reading. We shall read expectantly, obediently, and reverently, listening for His voice as Samuel did. "Speak, Lord, for Thy servant heareth" (1 Samuel 3:9). We shall be careful to put in that "Lord" which little Samuel inadvertently omitted! The Bible will thus make of that hour a fellowship with God.

It Begets Faith

We shall not get far in the life of prayer without faith. This quiet occupation of our hearts with God's Word is one of the greatest contributory causes of this essential quality. You remember how the Holy Spirit taught Paul to write that "faith cometh by . . . the Word of God" (Romans 10:17).

The Subject of Our Faith

The subject of our faith is as wide and varied, as big and as little as the things we pray about. We are to take up an attitude of trust concerning "all these things"(Mathew 6:32–33).

The Object of Our Faith

The object of our faith is God Himself. Whatever be your definition of faith, the meaning of it in the spiritual and Christian sense is a trusted God. It is an absolute confidence in the love and wisdom and power of Him to Whom you bring "all these things," that so far as the "good things" are concerned, He will withhold none such from you (Psalm 84:11). So far as the "bad things" are concerned, He will mold them for your good (Romans 8:28).

It is the Word of God that brings us to this happy confidence. Inasmuch as it is of such importance that we have this trust before ever we begin to pray about "all these things," we realize the necessity of beginning our prayer time with the Scriptures—letting Him speak to us before we ever speak to Him.

It Begets Knowledge

The very nature of the Word is light—"Thy Word is . . . light;" "The entrance of Thy words giveth light" (Psalm 119:105, 130).

Of Self

When we go to pray, the Bible will give us knowledge that will be invaluable to such an exercise of self. It will show us ourselves in real, true light. We must get that sight in order that we may ask to be put right.

Of Need

The Word will give us knowledge of need, not only of our own, but that of the people and the work for which we propose to pray. It gives knowledge not only of the superficial needs that we know of ourselves, but the fundamental needs that God's Word can reveal to us.

Of Him

The knowledge of Him is the knowledge above all other that we need and crave, and may have through the Word. Only those who really know God can ever become mighty prayer–warriors. So, let us ever seek the Word before we seek the Throne.

It Begets Worship

The actual word means worthship. His Word reveals His worth. It might be feared that the intimacy which He so graciously allows to men would lead to irreverence. But that would never happen with those who keep company with the Book. That precious volume leads us on to know Him, and to know is to worship.

It Begets Desire

For Ourselves

The Word begets desire for ourselves. The quiet and trustful meditation upon God's Word will awaken longings in our hearts that the things He has said to us may become actual in our experience—"quicken Thou

me according to Thy Word" (Psalm 119:25). The opening part of our prayer time will, in all likelihood, be a
turning of the portion into petition. If there was a promise, that we might receive it; if there was a warning, that
we might heed it; if there was a command, that we might
keep it; if there was an invitation, that we might accept
it; if there was a challenge, that we might take it; if there
was an ideal, that we might fulfill it. The Word is sure
thus to quicken our desire.

For Others

We shall be led on to intercession for so many, and
we shall assuredly find that our preliminary reading of
the Scriptures will shape and color our desires for them.

Our present study will have taught us that it is no
exaggeration to say that one of the greatest of all Prayer
Secrets is, begin with the Bible!

13

The Hands

"Pray everywhere, lifting up holy hands"
1 Timothy 2:8

The reference is to what was a common attitude of prayer: standing with hands stretched forth with empty palms toward heaven, as though waiting to receive in them the blessing sought for. And if those hands are really to obtain their desire, they must be holy. God will not place His pure gifts in dirty hands. The apostle is speaking figuratively. When he says hands, he means habits, and when he indicates habits, he is thinking of hearts. In other words, the hands are representative of the life. That must be right if we are to be successful in prayer, for what we are will always color what we ask. I imagine, however, that "holy hands" means something wider than just "clean hands," although that is the first and chief idea.

No Stain From Anything Committed

Our Hands Must Be Clean

"If I regard iniquity in my heart, the Lord will not hear me," says Psalm 68:18. So we see that our hands must be clean. There is a very remarkable passage in Isaiah

dealing with the sad fact that the people are utterly be-
reft of God's help and God's blessing. This is the expla-
nation given by the Lord Himself of that dreadful state
of affairs: "The Lord's hand is not shortened, . . . but
. . . your hands are defiled" (Isaiah 59:1-3).

God's hands were tied, because their hands were dirty.
Alas, it is often so. We pray, but nothing happens, because our sin has brought about the impotence of om-
nipotence! Let us be quite clear about things that we are
all too often in danger of forgetting. Stained hands are
uplifted in vain. God will not listen to the prayers of
sinful men and women. Yes, there is one prayer He will
heed, even from such. It is, "Wash me, and I shall be
whiter than snow" (Psalm 51:7).

Our Hands Can Be Cleansed

This reminds us that our hands can be cleansed. That
same man tells us in another place, "I will wash mine
hands in innocency" (Psalm 26:6). That must be done if
ever we are to be heard in the Audience Chamber. God's
petitioners can never do without the cleaning office and
cleansing operation of the Spirit and the Word and the
Blood. If it is essential to lift up holy hands, then thank
God that this is possible. Every stain of committed sin
can be washed away. I believe the Jews always washed
their hands before praying, but that outward ceremonial
can only be a symbol. The real thing is the cleansing of
the heart, the purifying of the life.

No Slur From Anything Omitted

We are often forced to confess that while we have done things that we ought not to have done, we have also left undone things we ought to have done. It has been said in reference to the text that heads this study that "holy hands" are hands which have committed no impiety, and which have observed every sacred duty.

Be it borne in mind that a slur is cast on our hands, on our hearts, by every wrongful omission.

Loss of Power in Prayer

Where there are duties left out, we lose power in prayer. Many a time, when people have been engaged in prayer, they have been wasting their energies and could have employed them to much better advantage by going about those ordinary duties that they have neglected.

Household duties or business engagements may be, in certain circumstances, of weightier obligation than the prayer meeting. God is not pleased with our attendance at the meeting if it has been made possible only by the work which is our plain duty being left or scamped! That sort of thing has cast a slur on the reputation and on the witness and on the experience of not a few believers, and has quite definitely brought discredit upon the Master's Name. Such God will not hear.

Presence of Power

Where there are no duties left out, we have such power in prayer. That is a very remarkable word that is given through John, "whatsoever we ask, we receive of Him, because we keep His commandments, and do those things that are pleasing in His sight" (1 John 3:22). When the hands are busily occupied in doing whatever God has required us to do—whether the things to be done be spiritual or secular—then, in that respect, they are "holy hands." They may be lifted up in prayer with happy expectancy.

No Scar From Anything Permitted

I do not think I am straining the point to add that there is to be no scar from anything permitted. Things committed may be inimical to prayer. Things omitted may be inimical to prayer. Things permitted, though perhaps not wrong in themselves, may be inimical to prayer. Such things always leave a scar on the life, on the hands.

True Behavior Brings Prayer Power

True behavior brings power in prayer, as we have already learned, and as the Master underlines for us again in John 15:16, "Bring forth fruit . . . that whatsoever ye shall ask of the Father in my Name He may give it you."

Doubtful Behavior Brings

Weakness in Prayer Power

Doubtful behavior is a source of weakness in prayer. To "abide" in the Vine brings certain success (John 15:7), but to wander in a doubtful place is the cause of many a barren prayer life.

Let us see to it that no doubtful indulgences are permitted in our lives, that the "hands," without stain, without slur, without scar, may be "holy." That is indeed a great Prayer Secret.

A little while ago I was out to tea with a family, and just as we sat down to the table, mother said to her little son, "Let me look at your hands." Sad to relate, they were not in a fit state to receive the good things of that table. But it was quite easy, and in the circumstances, well worthwhile, to go and wash them.

Do you think that, when we come to the laden Table of His glorious supplies, He first says to us, "Let Me look at your hands"? "He that hath clean hands" (Psalm 24:4) is the rule of the Household on the Hill. If we hope to obtain, our hands—that is, our hearts, our lives—must be cleansed from any defilement of commission, omission, or permission.

14

The Dew

"Be ready in the morning"—Exodus 34:2

The time for prayer is as varied as the circumstances of God's people. At any time, and at all times, we may call upon Him. Daniel had "three times a day" (Daniel 6:10), and David, "seven times a day" (Psalm 119:164). The point is that we all simply must have some time—a regular, specified time. "Any time" easily becomes "no time."

What, then, is the best time? In the generality of cases I have no hesitation in saying, "Be ready in the morning." There are exceptions for whom this is not practical, but for most of us it is not only possible but infinitely desirable.

The Freshness of the Morning Hour

Has the Dew

The morning hour has the dew. The dusty, musty atmosphere of the past day is changed to newness and charged with freshness. There is a feeling in the air that makes you decide, after all, it's good to be alive. It may be a wrench to leave your warm, comfortable bed, but when the effort has been made, the effect has been delicious! Is it not good to link up our time with God with such a time of the day?

Is the Dew

When that is done, such a time is the dew. It acts in the spiritual life as the ordinary dew does in the physical world. I have sometimes heard of people coming down cross and irritable to breakfast, but they are not those whose custom it is to rise in time for quiet with God. That habit tones up the spiritual system (and even the physical system) for the whole day.

The Fitness of the Morning Hour

The evening hour and the noonday hour may have an appropriateness of their own for prayer. At no hour is it out of place. But the early morning is peculiarly fitting for this holy employment, and that for several good reasons.

It is Free From Other Duties

There are duties, secular, material, domestic, official, which fall to us. But at this early hour they have probably not begun, and we shall be able to give our minds to the one duty and delight of prayer.

It is Not Likely to be Interrupted

The morning hour is not as likely to be interrupted as are the later periods of the day. And if our quiet time is to be effective and enjoyable, it is almost essential that we should be able to feel reasonably sure that nothing and no one will come bursting in to spoil it.

It is Right to Have the First

Appointment With God

It is surely right that our first appointment of the day should be with God—that we should listen to Him before anyone else, that we should speak to Him before anyone else. He is so gracious as to give us this early appointment, and He will be there to keep it. How more than ungracious on our part if we keep Him waiting, or even fail to show up. Whatever the cost, we must keep true.

Committing the Whole Day to God

It is possible in the morning to commit the whole day to God. When the day has already run part of its course, there is just much upon which God's blessing has not been sought. Each new day is a gift from God. We want to use it to the very most, and to the very best. Each new day is a fresh page in life's diary. We want to keep it clean and well written. Each new day is an unknown adventure. We want to meet it hopefully and unafraid. Each new day is another milestone on the road. We want to pass it with unfaltering tread and with head well back and with eyes aglow. Yes, all this and more is in it. If the day, with all its responsibilities and opportunities and anxieties is to be well lived, it must be committed to God "in the morning." For so many reasons we see the fitness of the early hour for holding blessed conversation with our God.

The Fruitfulness of the Morning Hour

The Quality of Disposition it Cultivates

It is interesting to observe the results of keeping the early watch. Note the quality of disposition it appears to cultivate. Have you not sometimes marked a delightful freshness about some Christians? They carry through a very full program, yet they never seem to get dull and stale, either in manner or in speech. This is, in almost every case, the outcome of that early Dew.

Have you noticed in some Christians a fine steadiness of demeanor, even in the midst of difficulty? R.L. Stevenson has a story of a boat in a terrible storm. The passengers were all driven below, and the tempest raged so fiercely that even the Captain had to be tied to his bridge. At last, one of the passengers, unable to endure the strain, crawled up on to the deck, and the sight he saw steadied his nerves and sent him back to his companions with the reassuring message, "It's all right. I have seen the Skipper's face." That is why some Christians can keep calm and strong and steady in spite of life's storm and stress. In the early morning they have seen the Captain's face!

The Caliber of Character it Seems to Produce

Read through the list of names—Charles Simeon, Samuel Rutherford, Robert Murray McCheyne, Earl Cairns, John Wesley, Martin Luther, and (to take one from modern times), C.T. Studd. Spiritual giants, every one of them. How did they reach that stature? Their own testimony would be: the early morning with God. If, for any reason, you cannot get this time, He will not allow you to suffer from its absence. But, that apart, I do not believe that anyone can attain this caliber of real spiritual greatness who does not begin early with the Master, up on the Mount.

The Measure of Personality it Encourages

There isn't much in some people—just what is on the surface—no depths. With other Christians it is so different. Whenever you meet them you find they have something to give—some blessing, some word, some radiance. Yes, they got it early that morning, when they were not only enriched themselves, but they received something extra to carry away for others.

When a believer was asked if the Resurrection were true, he replied, "Yes, I met Him this morning." That explains everything. Make no mistake about it, we have been touching a wonderful Prayer Secret here.

15

The Secret

"The secret of the stairs"
Song of Solomon 2:14

When I wrote out the title of this chapter, I did not intend that there should be any special emphasis on that "the." And yet, now that I come to think of it, as we are considering Prayer Secrets, I am not at all sure. Although I am not here using the word in that sense, perhaps we shall discover that the big Secret here revealed is *the* secret above all others, of provoking the prayer spirit. "The secret of the stairs," then, lies in several things.

A Secret Name

The Intimacy of that Name

We must think first of the intimacy of that name, "My dove." Over and over again we have sung about, "Jesus, lover of my soul," and that is perhaps one of the keys to the interpretation and understanding of this Song of Solomon. I feel that we must not say that it is the only key, but it is certainly one of the avenues to a grasp of the meaning of the book. It is His love for His Bride the church, and inferentially, His love for the individual believers who, together, make up the church. For all such, here is His secret name—what intimate love is suggested by it.

The Implications of that Name

Don't forget the implications of that name—that is, the nature that should characterize those who bear the name. It is a holy nature, for the dove is a very fastidious creature. It is an affectionate nature, for the dove has the nestling quality of true love. It is a soaring nature, for the dove, like all birds, has the habit of surmounting the things of earth and moving in the realm of heavenly things. It is a gentle nature, for the dove possesses that beautiful quality supremely. It is a spiritual nature, for the dove is peculiarly associated with the Holy Spirit (Mark 1:10). All these things are to be seen in each of us who is so enormously privileged as to be addressed by the Secret Name.

A Secret Refuge

I dare say you have read stories of mystery whose solution has lain in a concealed button, a sliding panel, a secret staircase, and an unsuspected hiding place. All very interesting. But don't forget that the spirit has a secret refuge, as our verse in the Song reminds us—"in the clefts of the rock."

Another familiar hymn drives home the wondrous truth: "Rock of Ages cleft for me, Let me hide myself in Thee."

How the Rock Came to be Cleft

We always remember how the Rock came to be cleft. I write a capital "R" because, as 1 Corinthians 10:4 tells us, "that Rock was Christ." His death for us sinners is typified by that smitten rock from whose cleft the life-giving stream emerged in the wilderness (Exodus 17:6). Christ was cleft by the Cross, and all who hide in Him are eternally safe and spiritually satisfied.

When the Rock Comes to be Trusted

Indeed, what rich blessedness accrues when the Rock comes to be trusted. There is an Old Testament passage which, by the vehicle of this same figure, teaches us how secure is our secret refuge in God. It is Exodus 33:21–22, where God tells Moses, "there is a place by Me," and bids him mount up to it and take his position "on the rock," and "in the rock." What security—"on" Him, and what refuge—"in" Him! That is where the secret of the stairs leads us.

A Secret Interview

Another aspect of their secret is that they are mounted for the purpose of a secret interview. Listen! The Lord is speaking—"let Me see thy countenance, let Me hear thy voice." This is where we touch upon the most amazing aspect of the prayer life. It is so amazing as to be well-nigh unbelievable—that He not only allows us to come, and invites us to come, and commands us to come, and empowers us to come, but that He actually longs for us to come! It can be for no personal attraction in ourselves.

The miracle is inexplicable unless on the ground of Sovereign Grace! "Jesus, what didst Thou find in me, That Thou hast dealt so lovingly?" is the amazed inquiry of the understanding saint.

He Finds Comeliness in Our Presence

Israel was reminded in Deuteronomy 10:15 that, "the Lord had a delight in thy fathers"—not because they were perfect, but because He was. Shall we try to grasp this extraordinary fact, that every time we miss our prayer time, He is strangely yet grievously disappointed! Surely, if anything were calculated to keep us eagerly anticipating the experience, it is the remembrance of this marvel. That we should find comeliness in His presence is nothing but inevitable truth. But that He should discover any comeliness in ours is a miracle of grace. Yet, nonetheless, it is gloriously the case!

He Finds Sweetness in Our Prayers

"The prayer of the upright is His delight," we are told in Proverbs 15:8. It is not merely that He promises to hear them and desires to hear them, but that He loves to hear them. Let the words and the tone of His appeal, "Let Me hear thy voice," only get hold of your heart, and I believe you will have no more difficulty about getting up in the morning. With unaccustomed alacrity you will be mounting "the secret . . . stairs."

A Secret Exhilaration

The Feet Will Move Happily

Life downstairs will be irradiated by our secret communion. The feet will move happily, for we shall "be . . . like . . . a young hart," as verse 17 of our passage suggests to us. If the skies be black and the air be sultry and the way be rough, it is not easy to move like that. But a hart is accustomed to the rough going of the mountains. Our feet will not drag so heavily, however difficult the path, if the time in the Secret Place is real enough to exhilarate our being.

The Face Will Glow Happily

The face will glow happily, even as we read of Moses that "the skin of his face shone" (Exodus 34:29–30), when he had been up on the mountain with God. It is a part of the blessing of "the secret . . . stairs," that we descend with such a prospect.

16

The Wrestler

*"Epaphras . . . always labouring fervently
for you in prayers"—Colossians 4:12*

The prayer experience is a varied one. Sometimes the
answer is gained easily, and at other times only after much
striving. He who would covet to be an effectual man of
prayer must be ready to wrestle, as did Epaphras.

A Great Love

Underneath that conflict of intercession there was a
great love. There will be no real wrestling without it. We
are not prepared to take such pains, to suffer such pains,
unless we do truly love. Paul says of this man, in verse
13, "I bear him record, that he hath a great zeal for you,
and them that are in Laodicea, and them in Hierapolis."
You see, so far as Colosse was concerned, there were
very close bonds uniting them to this Epaphras.

He Was One of Them

Epaphras was one of them ("one of you," verse 12). Natural kinship should always pass, through deep love, into spiritual concern. Evangelistic zeal should always begin at home, as Andrew's did, who "first findeth his own brother . . . and brought him to Jesus" (John 1:41–42).

He First Preached Christ Among Them

Then, he was the one who first preached Christ among them. The early verses of the first chapter of this epistle seem to convey that impression. Those Colossian believers were, in all probability, Epaphras' children in the faith. That gave them an added preciousness in his eyes.

He Was the One To Whom They Turned

He was the one to whom they turned so much for help, and guidance, and encouragement in all the difficulties of their new–begun Christian life, in their heathen surroundings. He was not with them at the time when Paul sent them this letter. If they were greatly missing him, he was no less greatly missing them! He was accustomed to do so much for them, but now, separated by hundreds of miles across land and sea as he is at Rome, what can he do for them? Love can always find something to do for its loved ones. Distance cannot prevent this man doing for them the greatest thing that anyone can do for another, so he prays for them.

A Great Aim

His prayer has a great aim—"That ye may stand perfect and complete in all the will of God."

Prayer for their Circumstances

It is a prayer for their circumstances, that "all the will of God" for them may be brought into actuality in their experience. His prayer is that they may miss none of it, that it may "all" enter into their life, even though at times it may seem untoward. Whatever is His will for us must also be His best for us. That covers not only our spiritual state, but also our physical and material conditions.

Prayer for their Steadfastness

Then, too, this is prayer for their constancy—"that ye may stand." It is prayer that no devilish influence in that pagan city shall bring about their moral downfall, that no painful experiences shall cause them one moment's doubt of the wisdom and love of the will of God, that no false teachers shall ever shake their firm grip of the truth, that nothing shall ever cause them to waver in their loyalty to their Lord.

Prayer for their Character

Perhaps we may also add that this is prayer for their character—"perfect and complete." It is prayer that may be ideally developed, and that they may be entirely filled. As this loving–hearted Epaphras thinks about his spiritual family, this is something of his ardent desire for them. This is the aim that he sets before him as he prays for them. It may well be our purpose to give ourselves to prayer for those on our list.

A Great Cost

Let it be noted that the prayer of Epaphras was made at a great cost. Here is one of the great Prayer Secrets, for what costs counts!

Great Expenditure of Time

If we go back to that verse 12 again, we find there was a great expenditure of time. He was "always" at it. For this grand purpose he took whatever time there was, and made whatever time there was not. Oh, that we knew more about this sacrificial giving of time to go apart with God to intercede for others. How infinitely worthwhile it would prove to be. It might involve us in the loss of some ease, some pleasure, some sleep perhaps. But what remunerative gains would be added to our "treasures in heaven" (Matthew 6:20).

Great Expenditure of Strength

It was more than time that Epaphras gave. There was also a great expenditure of strength. The word translated here "laboring fervently" is that from which our word "agony" comes, and it is the word used for the extreme exertions of the wrestler. Paul says, in effect, that as he marks his friend's earnest anguish in prayer, he can only liken it to a wrestler's toil and struggle. "With strong great wrestlings souls are won," as Horatius Bonar said in one of his hymns.

Do we know anything of prayer of this sort? All too

often we grow tired of praying, but do we ever grow tired through praying? Have we known often what it means to rise from our knees exhausted? You remember Jacob, wrestling at Peniel, and daring to say up into the face of God, "I will not let Thee go, except Thou bless me" (Genesis 32:26). How costly was his struggle. He went lame all his days, but he got him a new birth, a new name, a new power, a new day.

Let us seek His grace to learn the secret of wrestling prayer, at whatever cost to ourselves, a secret so mighty as to give power to prevail with God and with men.

A Great Need

The Lack of this Quality

Here is disclosed to us a great need—the grace of stickability. The lack of this quality is only too common and apparent even in Christian service. What constant need we find to urge believers to "keep on keeping on." Yet, he that putteth "his hand to the plough" of wrestling intercession and keeps "looking back" is no fit employee for the Kingdom (Luke 9:62).

The opposing forces of wind and rain may beat in his face, but he must "steadfastly set his face," as his Master did in another furrow (Luke 9:51).

The Secret of this Quality

The secret of this quality is, like all Christian virtues and graces, to be found "in the Spirit." It is as He is allowed absolute control of our being that we are enabled thus to wrestle in prayer "with all perseverance" (Ephesians 6:18). What a mighty Prayer Secret is here!

17

The Sky-Telegram

"So I prayed"—Nehemiah 2:4

Here is a kind of prayer that we have not so far considered, but it is one that all who believe in prayer should seek to become skilled in—the brief, momentary, ejaculatory utterance of our need. This may be called prayer in the form of a telegram, while the ordinary sort is in letter form.

Nehemiah was expert in both. Verse 4 of chapter 1 says, "I . . . prayed before the God of heaven." Verse 4 of chapter 2 says, "I prayed to the God of heaven." But the two prayers were so different in form. In the first case, he had plenty of time and opportunity to speak at some length and in detail, as if writing a letter. But in the other instance, he had no time nor chance for anything more than just a sentence—as it were, a telegram.

I think before we go any further, we ought to say that this type of prayer is only fully effectual when it is used by those whose believing habit it is to pray the ordinary way. That is, it is the men and women of prayer to whom the sky-telegram comes so readily and yields so rich a reward. Because Nehemiah had formed the splendid habit of regular prayer, as his whole story shows, he found it only natural to adopt this method of emergency prayer. He found also, we may be sure, abundant answers from his God.

A Sudden Need

Unsuspected Danger

All of this presupposes a sudden need. It may be some unsuspected danger. All in a flash the peril was upon us, for these things happen like that. One moment everything was right and bright, the next that horrid affair loomed up! At such a time, there is no chance for long prayer. The only thing to help is a sky–telegram.

Unforseen Temptation

Perhaps it is some unforeseen temptation. The temptation that we are aware of, and that we can prepare for, is difficult enough to deal with. But what shall we say of that which, without the slightest warning, comes upon us with all its lure and fascination, and with all its insidious appeal to some hideous weakness in our hidden nature? There is only one way of countering such, but thank God there is a way. 1 Corinthians 10:13 calls it "a way to escape." It is the sky–telegram.

Unexpected Opportunity

We may possibly have some unexpected opportunity, and the big emergency problem is, how thus instantaneously to use the chance to the most, and to the best. That was Nehemiah's situation. Sad as he was about the dreadful condition of his beloved city, and wondering however things could be put right, and how he himself could help towards it, the king suddenly shot the question at him, "What do you want me to do?" What a magnificent chance! What shall he ask for, how shall he use his opportunity? In all the excitement and possibility of the moment, he is man of God enough, he is man of prayer enough to see the utility of the sky–telegram.

A Swift Action

What a glorious Prayer Secret it is. For in such circumstances as we have described, it is obvious that the essential thing is swift action. Such needs will not wait for their solution.

No Time for Planning

There is no time for planning. If we had time to think the matter out, we might be able to evolve some scheme to meet it, whether it be danger, or temptation, or opportunity. But that is the whole point—there is no time to plan.

No Chance for Delay

Moreover, there is no chance for delay. Some things can be put off, but we are thinking just now of those things that cannot thus be dealt with. We cannot set them aside for consideration or for action when we are less flustered or less weak or less occupied. They will not allow us respite for a more convenient season. We must act now—now at once.

No Opportunity for Counsel

To add to our difficulties we have no opportunity for consultation. There are friends, perhaps, to whom we always take our troubles and our problems. We find that they always help so much. But the particular kind of emergency that we are here envisioning prevents all that. It must be faced and settled immediately and alone. How glorious it is, then, to remember that however swift the action demanded, there is always time for a sky–telegram.

A Short Message

Brevity

This implies a short message. It is of the very essence of a telegram that there be brevity. Sometimes the way is "Take with you words" (Hosea 14:2). But the occasions we are contemplating require, "let thy words be few" (Ecclesiastes 5:2).

There was an emergency in Peter's life when he only had time for a wire. Circumstances demanded that he should carefully count and cut his words to the minimum—"Lord, save me" (Matthew 14:30). Have we all tried a sky–telegram in sudden temptation? Peter's very words would admirably suffice. Don't wire for strength to save yourself, but for Him to save you from it.

Urgency

Another point of the telegram is urgency. How truly that was the case with Nehemiah. He had many problems and difficulties in the course of his life, but never a more urgent moment than this. So important was the issue that he dared to keep the King waiting for a reply until he had dispatched his wire and got back an answer!

May our study teach us to use more often the great Prayer Secret of the sky–telegram. And inasmuch as we shall never know when we shall suddenly need to send off one of these wires, we thank God that the G.P.O.— the Great Prayer Opportunity—is always open!

18

The Persistence

"Go again seven times"—1 Kings 18:43

What a great secret is here for the man and the woman of prayer. When James is dealing with the efficacy of prayer, he is led by the Holy Spirit to use this prophet Elijah as a great example of it. Lest we should be discouraged by a too-high illustration, he hastens to reassure us by reminding us that "Elias was a man subject to like passions as we are" (James 5:17). In other words, in spite of our weakness and difficulties we also can be prayer conquerors in God's Name. The particular point of the prophet's intercession that I want now to stress is its persistency—"go again," and again, and again. It is instructive to note the three stages in this story of an answer.

"There is Nothing"

"There is nothing"—that is the first report (verse 43). Indeed, that is the nature of the first six reports. Yet, are we quite sure there was nothing? Visibly, there was nothing, but really, was that so?

Nothing to be Seen

There was perhaps nothing to be seen, but then, never forget that God always does answer true prayer. Sometimes He says "Yes," and quite plainly and quite quickly the thing we ask for is in our hands. We greatly rejoice in His love. Sometimes He says "No," for the reason that He knows so well that the thing we ask for is not in our highest interests. In such cases, He takes care not to send us away empty, but He gives, in the place of our request, another thing. It is, as a matter of fact, a better thing. Sometimes He says "Wait," which is not to say that our prayer is unanswered, but only that the time for the positive answer is not ripe.

Something, to be Sure

We repeat, perhaps there is nothing to be seen, yet something, to be sure. Even the waiting will do something, if it is trustful. Put yourself in Elijah's place. What will that sixfold "nothing" do for him? Will it not make him increasingly distrustful of himself, and will it not make him absolutely dependent upon God? Is that "nothing"? If your prayers seems to go unanswered, still go on praying. The waiting will throw you back upon God. Besides, an objective answer will assuredly come in His time and way.

"There Ariseth a Little Cloud"

An Impression in Heaven

"There ariseth a little cloud," says verse 44. So his

prayer has made an impression in heaven. "Like a man's hand," is the servant's description of the shape of that little cloud. The fact seems rather particularly to have impressed the man, or there would have been no reason to mention it. The prophet's hand, uplifted as his heart, had been so eager, so importunate, that it could almost be said to have stamped itself upon the sky.

An Impression on Us

As we think of it, we are constrained to ask, shall his prayer not make an impression upon us? It is the lesson of continuance that we so greatly need to learn. That is another of the great Prayer Secrets that we are seeking to discover. Whatever may be the delays, the difficulties, the disappointments, the discouragements, don't stop praying. Sooner perhaps than we realize, there will arise "a little cloud." Over and over again our Master taught in one way or another that men "ought always to pray [to keep on at it] and not to faint," (Luke 18:2) as we see in the parable of the unjust judge. Again, in the parable of the friend at midnight in Luke 11:5 we see it—don't stop praying. Sooner or later, your Friend will send you the answer that shall enable you to be a friend to your friend. If that be the impression left upon us, we shall have learned a big secret of prevailing intercession. Look out for the "little cloud."

"There Was a Great Rain"

The Scale of Earth's Need

"There was a great rain" in verse 45. Let us remind

ourselves that that is the scale of earth's need. After three years of drought, nothing "little" will satisfy. Only what is "great" will suffice.

As we look about the world in our day, the spiritual need is truly tremendous: the decadence of morals, the desecration of God's day, the disregard of God's Word, the deadness of so much professing Christianity. Such things cause God's people to cry out from the very depths of their hearts, "Wilt Thou not revive us again?" (Psalm 85:6).

If we have been to God about this and "there is nothing," then let the prophet inspire us to "go again, seven times," persisting until the "great rain" comes.

The Scale of Heaven's Giving

This is the scale of heaven's giving. There is nothing little about your God. "The Lord is great," says Psalm 96:4, and "the works of the Lord are great," adds Psalm 111:2. So be quite sure if you get "a little cloud," and a few drops, that is only just a sample. You are not to rest content with that, not to be satisfied until you have "a great rain."

There is something wrong about the hymn which says, "Lord, I hear of showers of blessing . . . Let some droppings fall on me." Who wants droppings, when showers are to be had? Here is a mighty secret. Keep on at it, for the reward of persistency is not "little" but "great"!

Repeatedly in the course of these studies we have stressed this quality of persistence, for the reason that we do so easily give up. Suppose Elijah had given up.

Suppose he had allowed the six-fold delay to discourage him into saying that it was no good praying for rain any more!

How earnestly the hearts of many of God's people are longing today for that other rain—revival. Who knows but that we may be even at "the sixth time." Whatever happens (or does not happen), don't let us give up now. Give God His due (Malachi 3:10) and "give Him no rest" (Isaiah 62:7). Perhaps, before we are much longer on our knees, the windows of heaven may be opened and we may have "a great rain." And if not, let us not be foiled of the blessing. Let us "go again seven times"—yea, seventy times seven!

19

The Underground

"Helping together by prayer"
2 Corinthians 1:11

We are accustomed in these days to the idea of underground shelters and underground passages, and even underground railways. But what will you say to the idea of underground prayer?

The Construction of a Word

Let me invite your attention to the construction of a word. "Helping together," is one word in the Greek. It is a most interesting word and throws a great deal of light upon the whole subject of prayer.

The Root Word

There are three parts to this word. Part one is the main root of the word, meaning "work." Now it is a good thing at the outset to get a real grasp of the fact that prayer actually is work. Some Christians may be heard bemoaning that they cannot do any work, they can only pray! But that is work. Indeed, it can be very hard work and is certainly very fruitful work. Let there be no mistake about it—some of the finest and most effective Christian work is done by bedridden invalids who can "only pray"!

The Particle

Part two is a little particle which means "with." The idea which is thus added is that prayer is fellowship—a working with. Paul is at work in Philippi when he writes this letter. He asks the brethren at Corinth, by their prayers, to cooperate with him in his work. It is like Moses and Joshua at the battle of Rephidim (Exodus 27:8). The one is on the mountain, the other in the valley. The former does the praying, the latter does the fighting. They were working together. Note that the prayer part of the partnership appears the more potent, for when it slackens the fighting lacks success!

Another Particle

Part three is another little particle, which, in such combination, means "underneath." So that the full conception of this fascinating word is that prayer (among many other things) is a working together underneath—an underground weapon!

The Contemplation of this Force

In World War I (1914–1918), the key position of Messines Ridge was taken by the Allied Armies through the effective combination of forces. The gunners and the airmen were at work up above, and the engineers were working together underneath. For some while these latter had been tunneling beneath the Ridge, laying the wires and the dynamite, so that when the moment arrived, the pressing of a button blew the Ridge sky high.

The Gospel is described as a high explosive. In Romans 1:16 the Holy Spirit actually leads Paul to use a word which our Authorized Version translates "power," and which is the very word from which our word "dynamite" comes.

In laying siege to Mansoul, prayer's underground work can gloriously prepare the way for the laying of the dynamite of the Gospel, which can blow souls right side up and propel them to the skies. What a wonderful force it is.

How Far It Can Go

By this means we can tunnel to Africa, or China, or India, or South America, or anywhere else we choose.

How Much It Can Do

Even those who are completely disinterested and would normally give no attention to the things of God can be stung into giving heed as the Holy Spirit convicts them in response to our underground activities.

How Strong It Can Be

There are those to be won who are not merely disin-terested, but are positively antagonistic. They would never dream of allowing you to speak to them about God. But they cannot prevent you speaking to God about them. This underground procedure has many a time been found to have broken down all opposition. The more we con-template this mighty force, the more inclined we are to take up the Secret Weapon more than ever.

The Concentration of this Method

Let us encourage one another still further by looking at an illustration. It was one of the most thrilling occa-sions in Peter's adventurous career. Indeed, it seemed to be the end of his career.

The Situation He Faced

What a situation he was in. "Peter . . . was . . . in prison," Acts 12:5 tells us. In the morning he was to be brought out to his execution. He had been incarcerated before and had escaped (Acts 5:19). Taking no chances this time, the authorities had taken every possible pre-caution. They did not know how he had got out last time, but this time it shall be made absolutely impossible. Chained to a couple of soldiers in the cell, two more posted sentry-wise outside the cell door, all the gates securely fastened—no help could reach poor Peter now! Except, of course, underground. And the authorities had never thought of that, "but prayer was made."

What a Surprise They Got

What a surprise they all got. As for the guards—"as soon as it was day, there was no small stir among the soldiers, what was become of Peter," (verse 18). They may be excused, for they knew nothing about this Secret Weapon of Underground Prayer. What I do find strange (until I recall my own all too frequent lack of faith) is that the prayer meeting was so surprised "when they . . . saw him, they were astonished" (verse 16). Certainly they should have known better, but in fact, everybody is surprised by the wonderful results of a concentration upon this Prayer Secret.

The Continuation of this Story

It is not the carrying on with the story of Peter that I am thinking of, although that would be a most profitable study in the wider and subsequent results of the "underground" method. It is the personal continuance of the story of the Secret Weapon that I have in mind. Tunneling to foreign lands—what blessing we might bring to tired and discouraged workers, what new accessions of strength and hope and courage, what triumphs of the Gospel we might enjoy, even though separated by such distances from them. Tunneling next door—to reach those neighbors who it seems can be touched in no other way. They just can't keep you out if you go underground by prayer.

Shall we continue the story by adding thus fresh chapters to the adventures and victories of this way? For example—let us be definite and practical—shall we start on our neighbors at once?

20

The Harmony

"When ye stand praying, forgive, if ye have aught against any"—Mark 11:25

I have a kind of idea that in touching upon this subject I am dealing with a very frequent cause of failure, not only in the sphere of private prayer, but also in the case of the prayer meeting. Repeatedly, an unforgiving spirit has atrophied prayer power. It would be a Prayer Secret well learned if we could see this and put this right.

No Effective Prayer

Without Harmony

On Terms With Him

There can be no effective prayer without harmony

with Him. We must be on terms with Him. In "At the Sixtieth Milestone," the late greatly beloved and honored Dr. Fullerton tells a story which exactly makes this point. Old Mrs. Cobley used to visit Leicester Infirmary with flowers. One day a young doctor met her coming out of a ward and in a frolicsome mood asked, "Well, Mrs. Cobley, I suppose you have been telling these people that God hears prayers?" "Yes, sir," she answered. "My Father always hears people when they cry." "I am very glad to hear it," he replied, "for I am very hard up this morning. Do you think that if I asked your Father for a five-pound note He would give it to me?" That was a bit of a stumper, for "yes" or "no" would have been equally wrong. At last she said, "Suppose you were introduced to the Prince of Wales today, sir. Do you think that the first day you knew him you could ask him for a five-pound note?" "No, I suppose I would need to wait until I got to know him better." "Yes," finished the old lady in triumph, "and you will need to know my Father better before you can ask Him for five-pound notes." That makes our first point clear, doesn't it?

In Tune With Him

Let me add that we must be in tune with Him. Our lives, our desires, our wills must be adjusted to His mind. As we saw earlier, that is asking "in His Name," and that is asking "according to His will."

No Harmony Without Pardon

Not Judicial Pardon

"That your Father . . . may forgive you your trespasses," is essential to harmony. There can be no such relationship without it. This is not here judicial pardon. That became ours the very moment we trusted Christ. It was given us on the ground of the propitiatory blood–shedding which "satisfied the law's demands." Without it we could never have entered the family and enjoyed "peace with God."

Paternal Pardon

This is paternal pardon. We have not now to do with the Judge, but with the "Father." Although Galatians 3:26 tells us we are in the family through faith, there may yet be trespasses. They do not mean our forfeiting the place in the family, but they do mean our losing the joy of the fellowship. When the children are disobedient, they are not dismissed from the home, but they are depressed in the heart. If harmony is to be restored we must have pardon from the Father. Until that harmony is restored, there can be no effectual prayer to the Father. So far the whole thing is self–evident.

No Pardon Without
Forgiveness of Others

Here are His words for it in verse 26 of the passage: "If ye do not forgive, neither will your Father . . . forgive your trespasses." Let it be repeated that this is not concerned with place in the family, but with peace in the family—a *sine qua non* of prayerful access to the Father. This works both ways.

"If ye have aught against any" (Mark 11:25)

Has that one cut you, insulted you, maligned you, injured you? Consequently, are you harboring a grudge? My friend, you must forgive quite sincerely and without any manner of reservation. They were in the wrong, yes, but that only makes it the greater privilege for you to be the one to get the matter put right. It is going to be very difficult, yes, but have you not the Holy Spirit abiding in you, and is it too difficult for Him? In any case, it has got to be done. You must forgive, that is, if you value your harmony with God and your power in prayer. If they do not respond to your advances, it can't be helped. You will have your reward, because you have done your part.

"If . . . thy brother hath aught against thee"
(Matthew 5:23)

This time it is you that is in the wrong. Even, perhaps, at the very moment that you come to offer your gift or your prayer, your conscience smites you and you are reminded of the wrong you have done that other. It is no use offering your gift or prayer. You must leave it for the moment untendered, while you go and ask his forgiveness. In cases where necessary and possible, you must make restitution. It will take some doing, for you must admit to being wrong, you must humble your pride, you must run the risk of being insulted. None of these things are easy, but we should have thought of all the wrong we did our brother. Again, if he will not receive our repentance, we shall at least have done our part. At any cost to ourselves we must go to him and seek reconciliation. The harmony with our fellows, which is essential to our harmony with God, in turn is a preliminary of a God–blessed prayer life.

No Forgiveness Without the Holy Spirit

The real forgiveness of personal slight and injury seems to be found very, very difficult. It appears to require a power stronger than we naturally possess. A word of singular appropriateness comes to us in Romans 5:5: "the love of God is shed abroad in our hearts by the Holy Ghost Who is given unto us." The original for "love" does not signify the ordinary natural affection, but a supernatural quality. It is a love which is strong enough and big enough to accomplish this happy triumph of forgiving people who have wronged us.

If We Possess the Holy Spirit

If we possess the Holy Spirit, that love–power is at hand. Every true believer, as Romans 8:9 makes clear, does possess Him from the moment of his new birth.

If The Holy Spirit Possesses Us

If the Holy Spirit possesses us, if day by day we are surrendered completely to His possession, if we are walking in obedience, then that supernatural power is positively set free to do its blessed work of love. The forgiving spirit is ours!

21

The Map

"Lift up your eyes, and look on the fields"
John 4:35

This present study will not be an exposition of the text, but just an application (not an illegitimate application, I hope). The believer's work of intercession is meant to have a very wide sweep. While he is, first and foremost, responsible for his own home, he is not intended to limit himself to that restricted sphere. He must launch out into his neighborhood and into his country, and indeed, into the whole wide world. If he cannot, in person, fulfill His Master's command to "Go . . . into all the world" (Mark 16:15), he can and must fulfill it in prayer. Being as every Christian must be, missionary–hearted, he will give time and strength in regular order, prayerfully to "look on the fields" in foreign lands.

This part of our petitions will be rendered more interesting, more intelligent, more vivid, more thrilling, and so, more effectual, by the definite use of the map. Your missionary society is certain to issue maps of its spheres of operation. But I would recommend you to use the maps of an ordinary atlas, onto which you have copied the more specific missionary detail in ink of an outstandingly distinctive color, to be seen at a glance.

So far as missionary intercession is concerned, I believe this would be found to be a grand Prayer Secret. With the map before us, then, let us lift up our eyes and take the prayer–look on the fields.

The Look that Grasps the Situation

We can never pray about missions to the best advantage unless we get the proper viewpoint. That is always to be had from a kneeling position. Take the trouble to acquaint yourself with the tricks of map reading, for this matter is of such high importance that it is worth taking pains. And now, on your knees, study the situation. Prayer will give you such a sympathetic understanding.

The Geographical Factor

Your good detailed atlas map will show you the hills and the valleys, the railways, perhaps the prevailing winds and temperatures, and a score of details that will help you to grasp the situation.

The Personal Factor

Your markings from the missionary magazines and reports will indicate how the men and women of the Gospel are placed, among vastly populated areas, or in lonely spots, together with certain facts about their schools, hospitals, churches, and compounds. To see these things on the map and to see them on our knees will give us the look that grasps. We shall be enabled to take it in, and so to pray.

The Look that Grapples with Difficulty

We do not need to be reminded that difficulties abound in the mission "fields." Perhaps we may say that they arise from three directions.

The Personality of the Missionary

He is no less human than we at home. He is sometimes a square peg in a round hole, and being "square," he may be "angular." He is constantly enduring the strain of heat, flies, and heathen atmosphere. Small wonder if he sometimes loses the concert pitch, and all the greater need that we should pray that the Psalmist's testimony, "All my fresh springs are in Thee" (Psalm 87:7), may be his constant experience. The map will help us to see something of this need.

The Personality of the Native

The personality of the native abounds with problems for those who, to him, are foreigners, and who bring to him a Gospel which he finds so foreign to his own thought and life. Misunderstandings and clashes are not surprising in all the circumstances. Our marked map will keep us wise to these difficulties and send us often to our knees.

The Personality of the Enemy

Just how vile, how revolting, how subtle, and how antagonistic he can be is seen nowhere so clearly as in his own strongholds in the heathen "fields" of the world. As we open our map before God, we can, on our knees, do battle with Satan in that particular field, there and then. If your map happens to be open that day at Africa, that country has an animal that could teach you something of deep value. It is the gnu. It has this most interesting and spiritually instructive habit. When it sights an enemy, it goes down onto its knees and springs to attack from its knees!

At the Keswick Convention at which these talks had their origin, the daily Bible readings were given by that great–hearted evangelist, Mr. Lionel Fletcher. He gave to his studies the challenging title, "Kneeling to Conquer"! I wonder if, in his worldwide wanderings, he has ever met the gnu? Such is the way to grapple with difficulties abroad or at home.

The Look that Greets
the Opportunity

The Master Saw Opportunity in Difficulty

To some folks, difficulty is always an opportunity, and that is always how it looks from our knees. The Master saw opportunity in difficulty. His disciples would say, "Four months," ploughing, sowing, waiting in those Samaritan fields. But, as He saw the crowd of inquirers coming from Sychar, He said, "Harvest already." The seed planted in the sinful woman's heart had as quickly produced a harvest.

The Apostle Saw Opportunity in Difficulty

Recall Paul's outlook in 1 Corinthians 16:9, "a great

door and effectual is opened unto me, and there are many adversaries." Most of us would have written "but," as if the enemies turned the opportunity into an impossibility. But he just says "and," as if those enemies are to be taken in his stride. Certainly he will not allow the difficulty to spoil the opportunity. So let your map show you the doors and the barriers, but "look on the fields" from the vantage point of your knees, and that look of prayer will do its own grasping, grappling, and greeting work.

The Look that Grips the Plan

Looking up from our kneeling attitude, we observe once more our glorious Ascending Lord, catching the very echoes of His voice that has just outlined His plan for the "fields" given in Acts 1:8.

The Missionary Member

"Ye"—every disciple is a missionary ex–officio!

The Missionary Mandate

"Shall be"—not of choice, not of fad, but of command. A Christian who affects to disbelieve in missions is a rebel!

The Missionary Method

"Witnesses"—just telling what we have personally come to know.

The Missionary Message

"Me"—what a message!

The Missionary Map

"In Jerusalem . . . Judaea . . . Samaria . . . uttermost parts of the earth." Prayer with the map grips that plan and looks further for the Holy Ghost power to help to carry it out.

22

The By-product

"They that wait upon the Lord shall renew their strength"—Isaiah 40:31

"By-product" is a term used for commodities produced incidentally in the course of some manufacturing process, the principal aim of which is another and generally quite different product. It forms one of the romances of industry. It includes some of our most useful things. For example, coke is a by-product of the manufacture of gas. Iodine is a by-product from nitrate workings.

Now I am going to suggest that the great quality of personal renewal is a by-product from the making of prayer. The real purpose of prayer is the securing of objective blessings. But in doing that it also produces, incidentally, a subject blessing upon the one who prays. You might be doing some work in the mountain air or sea air, and while the object of your labor was not your own health, yet you would find that, as an incidental result (a by–product), your health was the subject of some great improvement.

Our spiritual well–being, like the physical, demands good food, good air, and good exercise. The food is the Bible. The exercise is service. And the air is prayer. Whatever we accomplish on this mountain top, we are in any case ourselves refreshed and strengthened in our own souls by the glorious, invigorating air that ever sweeps around the throne of God. This explains why the great exemplars of prayer have always been such strong spiritual characters. This came to them as a by–product of their labors in prayer.

New Strength for Everybody

The Promise is for All

The passage itself makes it clear that the promise is for all. The "they" is to include every sort and condition—young and old, weak and strong, clever and dull, notable and insignificant, rich and poor, clerical and lay, male and female. The only limitation set is that they "wait upon the Lord." Whosoever comes within this category, of whatever character, color, or caliber, the promise of new strength is theirs.

The Need is Among All

There are some who will naturally tire and fail, while others would seem to be able to go on and on. Yet "even the youths... and the young men" stand in as great need as the rest of us of regular spiritual renewal. Whoever prays—really prays—shall have this benefit of prayer's by-product.

New Strength for Everything

"They shall mount up with wings as eagles; they shall run, and not be weary; they shall walk, and not faint." That three-speed gear covers all gradients of life's roadway.

The Outstanding Thing

There is first the mounting with wings. There is some demand upon us for exceptional endeavor, exceptional expenditure, and exceptional adventure. They are not every day occurrences. They are altogether out of the way of our usual routine, but the sudden call comes, the unexpected challenge is upon us, and we "needs must" take it up. God knows we shrink from it, but we cannot escape it. Now, he who habitually spends time on the mountain will find that he had taken in fresh strength that morning of the challenge, which will enable him to manage anything that God allows to come to him—even the exceptional thing, the outstanding thing.

The Onerous Thing

Then, there is running. That does not have the excitement of flying, but it takes heavy toll of wind and limb. Life, for some Christians, is a continuous and hard toil. They carry a heavy burden. Yet, they shall "not be weary" if they are accustomed to stretch their limbs, and open their lungs in the fresh breezes that blow around the crest of Mount Prayer.

The Ordinary Thing

Nor is forgotten the ordinary thing of walking. No thrill about this. It is but the humdrum of life, "the common round, the trivial task," day after day doing the same old thing, heel and toe, heel and toe! The very dullness of it has its danger. It often becomes uncommonly hard to keep going. Yet, if the people concerned have learned the value of our Prayer Secret, they shall "not faint."

So, for every kind of experience that may come to us, there is grace enough to meet it. There is ever an accession of sufficient strength to face it.

New Strength for Every Day

Yesterday's Strength Inadequate

The old word of Deuteronomy 33:25 says, "As thy days, so shall thy strength be." Yesterday's strength will not do, although not a few Christians try to manage on it.

They had a great refreshing at Keswick last July. They had a mighty time of uplift twenty-five years ago, and they are still living on that (certainly glorious) past experience. As if God's invigorating winds were twenty-five years old, or blew only in July, or were to be found only at Keswick. No, no. That won't do!

Tomorrow's Strength Not Yet Needed

Those who tearfully complain that they are afraid they have not "dying grace" will not get it until it is needed. God does not impart His fresh graces in advance to grow stale in our soul's cupboards. No need to worry about future supplies.

Today's Strength is Ours

I expect you took in a great store of it this morning, as a by–product, when you went to "wait upon the Lord." Martin Luther once said, "If I should neglect prayer but a single day, I should lose a great deal of the fire of faith.

New Strength for Everywhere

In so many ways we are creatures of our environment. Scientists have of later years come to hold that environment has a greater effect upon our individuality than heredity. Yet, in this passage of the promise of daily renewal, there is no mention of surroundings.

Spiritual Renewal in All Climates

It is as if spiritual renewal is suitable to all climates—the hot and the cold, the friendly and the hostile, the dry and the humid, the depressing and the exhilarating. Surely, the saints of Calcutta, Cariboo, and Copenhagen could all testify to the invigorating quality of this "waiting upon the Lord"—the same everywhere.

Spiritual Strength in All Demands

Let the situation of God's people be what it may,

whether physically, geographically, materially, or spiritually. The daily visit to the Throne will, in addition to any
other benefit obtained, greatly refresh their own souls.

23

The Receptacle

"When ye pray, believe that you receive
. . . and ye shall have"—Mark 11:24

The Prayer Secret at which we have now arrived is one which is fundamental to the whole matter, and essential to all success in it. It is the relationship between prayer and faith. Prayer is the request for a blessing.

Faith is the Vessel That

Retrieves the Blessing

"Believe . . . and ye shall have." This is the attitude that God is so glad to observe in us and the attitude that so greatly ministers to His glory.

Certain of Receiving

It is so sure of receiving that the thing asked for is already as good as ours. Dr. Scroggie tells of a visiting speaker who was so pleased with the answer of a boy in Sunday School that he promised the next day to send him a book. The youngster ran home in excitement and said, "Mother, I've got a book." When the mother asked, "Show it to me," he replied, "Oh, I haven't got it yet!"

No, he had not. Yet, he felt so sure of receiving it that he was talking as if he already had it.

Perhaps we may say that this is an application of the principle enunciated in Hebrews 11:13, which speaks of some who "in faith, not having received the promises . . . embraced them."

Certain to Receive

Such an attitude is so sure to receive, for it indicates so plainly that we trust God's promise, which is honoring to God, Who said, "Them that honor Me, I will honor" (1 Samuel 2:30). If we honor His word, He will honor our faith.

I can so well imagine that Sunday School boy saying to the speaker, as he left that Sunday afternoon, "Oh, I say, sir, thank you very much for the book." How could he disappoint such trust in his promise?

When Gipsy Smith began taking his little family to church, he taught them to bow their heads in prayer for God's blessing as soon as they had gotten to their seats. When he asked his eldest, on one occasion, what words he used, the little chap told his father that he said, "For what we are about to receive, the Lord make us truly thankful." Sure of receiving; sure to receive. So, as we ask, let us thank Him for the answer, being so sure of getting it. And let us act accordingly. As we come with our request, let us bring with us our receptacle of appropriating faith in which to bring home the blessing.

Faith is a Vessel That Retreives From Such a Fount of Blessing

Faith in the Promise

"Have faith in God," says verse 22 of Mark 11. We have been speaking just now about faith in the promise, and a right royal secret that is, for the promise will never fail us.

Evan Hopkins, the great Keswick teacher, was once consulted by a troubled soul. I do not remember what was the nature of the malady, but I do recall the nature of the remedy. That great soul-specialist recommended his patient to go to her room with her Bible and to have "half-an-hour's believing"! To seek out the promises, to note the conditions, and then quite simply to take them at their face value, this is enough to steady any unstable Christian. Such an absolute reliance upon His Word is a tonic, a dynamic thing.

Faith in the Promiser

It depends upon faith in the Promiser—not the thing, but the Person. It is not the Word, but the Speaker. When a distressed soul said to Dr. Torrey, "I can't believe," that incisive, clean-cut evangelist surprised him and revolutionized his whole life by replying, "Whom can't you believe?" Not "what," but "Whom." Is it so very hard to trust Him, so difficult to believe what He says? Come, come—"have faith in God." He is the Fount of Blessing where faith is encouraged to come and dip. What we receive from Him will be largely conditioned by what we perceive of Him. This brings me to the main emphasis.

Faith is a Vessel That Can Grow to Retrieve the Greatest Blessing

"What things soever ye desire," the Master gives, in our 24th verse, as the scope of His promise to the praying disciple. Even the removal of a mountain into the sea is not too much for the big faith that is here indicated.

Our Desire, His Will Coincide

The more we are occupied with, and the more we learn of the Promiser, the more will our desire and His coincide. It is not always His will to remove mountains. Sometimes He wishes us to surmount them. What a mountain of difficulty and seeming opposition to the progress of the Gospel was Paul's ill health. Yet it was not God's will that it should be removed, but that it should be surmounted (2 Corinthians 12:7–10). So, as we have said, the clearer our conception of Him and His desire, the greater will be our reception of our desires because they will be, growingly, His desires.

Our Desire Fulfilled

Yes, the more will our desire be fulfilled by the "God from Whom all holy desires, all good counsels, and all just works do proceed." Let us, then, see that our faith becomes a big enough thing to appropriate "what things soever" are inwrought in our desires by "God which worketh in you . . . to will . . . of His good pleasure" (Philippians 2:13).

During a very severe winter, the lady–bountiful of a

certain village said that on a particular day she would fill with warm, nourishing soup the jug of every inhabitant who applied. When the morning arrived, they all filed along to the big house with a jug which they had taken from the dresser. Sure enough, the jug was filled. But listen! One of the old dears came along with her big bedroom jug, and although the rest of them laughed at her, she stoutly maintained that no one had said anything about the size of the jug. Her faith was rewarded, for even as promised, her jug was filled. She received more because she believed more. So let our longing be "Lord, increase our faith" (Luke 17:5). May the receptacle grow increasingly. May we bring a big jug when we come to the inexhaustible Supply. And may faith be great enough to rejoice in the gift before it arrives, because we know the Giver Who made the promise to our prayers.

In a time of terrible drought, with not a cloud in the sky and no sign whatever of any change, some people in a village held a meeting to pray for rain. One person was laughed at because she took an umbrella to the meeting when the skies were cloudless! Yet, she was the truest Christian of them all. She not only believed that she received, but acted accordingly. Her large umbrella showed the reality of her faith. So perhaps we had better bring an umbrella as well as a big jug. Ask big—and act accordingly!

24

The Twin

"Prayer . . . with thanksgiving"
Philippians 4:6

The apostle is showing us the footsteps to peace. He says they are three in number: one, careful for nothing; two, prayerful for everything; and three, thankful for anything. It is this last that we are to think about now—thanksgiving, the very twin of prayer.

The Encouragement of the

Man in Prayer

Good Companions

I am going to suggest that we have here a case of good companions, for these two qualities go so naturally and happily together. "Prayers and Praises go in pairs; They have Praises who have Prayers." The one who engages in prayer should engage also in thanksgiving.

Good Business

When we pray, we have dealings with God in the business of the Kingdom. "Received with Thanks" plays an important part in any business. A house which neglected to send receipts would soon find itself losing business. It is wise to remember thanksgiving.

Good Manners

Having received the answer to our prayer, we should come back and say, "Thank You!" We recall the ten lepers who prayed so earnestly for cleansing and who, so lovingly and so wonderfully, were granted the healing they implored. One of the company returned with an expression of profoundest gratitude. One, yes, only one. "But where are the nine?" (Luke 17:17), asked their Divine Benefactor in pained remonstrance.

Is He not troubled afresh by the absence of this note of thanksgiving from many of our public prayer meetings and many of our private sessions of supplication? Oh, that He might find us more frequently engaged in this holy exercise.

The Encouragement of the Habit of Prayer

Prayer Has Been Answered

The thanksgiving which belongs to prayer is a great spur to go on in prayer, for it reminds us that prayer has been answered. There are abundant evidences to be drawn from the experience of God's servants all down the years that He does heed His people's cry. But, better still, we know that now from our own experience.

Prayer Will Be Answered

We have come for prayer thanksgiving, and that very fact inspires us to act on the assumption that prayer will be answered. We still have needs—problems, opportunities, dangers, sorrows, anxieties, and desires, so that we shall still continue to pray as those who "needs must." In any case, even though we had not those needs, we should keep on praying simply because we are told to do so. It would be undertaken as a matter of obedience.

But, what if we have prayer thanks to bring? Why then, how greatly and how expectantly we are encouraged to persevere in the habit. If there were nothing else to encourage us, it would be sufficient urge that our having a thanks at all is adequate indication of how worthwhile it always is to pray. That is what makes thanksgiving such a great Prayer Secret.

The Enrichment of the Life of Prayer

Prayer is Varied

If ours is in any real sense a life of prayer, we shall have discovered how varied an occupation prayer is. The late Dr. Alexander Whyte, that great master in the things of the spirit, has said that "Prayer is a comprehensive and compendious name for all kinds of approach and all kinds of address to God, and for all kinds and all degrees of communion with God."

Adoration, confession, petition, intercession, thanksgiving—all would be included. Thanksgiving would be so truly the twin of prayer as to be inseparable from it. In any case, how infinitely poorer would prayer be without it, and how infinitely richer if it is included!

Prayer is Interesting

How interesting prayer is when thanks is not absent. Some people have complained that they found prayer dull, and that they got quickly tired of it. That has never been the experience of those who have learned so effectually to pray that they have had specifically recognizable answers, for which they habitually bring their thanks. This latter makes the prayer life so rich in joy and hope.

The Environment of the
Way of Prayer

He who treads often in the way of prayer finds himself moving in the sunlit atmosphere of thanksgiving. A really prayerful man is a truly thankful man. Paul was a live example of that, for both those spirits abounded in him. Such a man's thanksgiving for answered prayer breeds in him a sense of thankfulness in general—"giving thanks always for all things," in Paul's own phrase (Ephesians 5:20).

Positive Answers Elicit Thanks

How abundant are the blessings of answered prayer. There is a familiar hymn of delightful and proper sentiment, which for its sheer impossibility greatly amuses me: "Count your blessings, name them one by one." How can you? Try it with pencil and paper and see how the list grows until you despair of finishing it.

Negative Answers Elicit Thanks

The things we have not gotten also call for thanks. Have you ever thought that every misery you haven't gotten is a mercy you have gotten! Oh yes, in the leanest times, in the darkest times, in the hardest times, we have so much to be thankful for, especially for all that prayer, real prayer, means. Such a thanks will be expressed to our gracious God "not only with our lips, but with our lives," for often the best thanksgiving is thanksliving.

Be careful never to separate the twins. They have a mutual effect upon each other which keeps them both in a thoroughly healthy condition. Prayer without thanks is likely to be a dull thing. Thanks without prayer is bound to be a delicate thing which cannot thrive. But both, in continual association, keep one another strong. Besides, thanksgiving is so good for our own souls, seeing that "a merry heart doeth good like a medicine," as Proverbs 17:22 says, and as every physician will agree!

25

The Example

"As He . . . us"—Luke 11:1

You remember how the apostle, writing under the inspiration of the Holy Spirit, speaks of our Lord Jesus as "leaving us an example, that ye should follow His steps" (1 Peter 2:21). That example covers the whole field of life and is nowhere more important than in the sphere of prayer. The Master said a great deal about the subject of prayer, but that is not to be our study just now. We are rather proposing to think not of His teaching, but of His practice.

The Regular Habit

There are no less than fifteen separate occasions on which He is mentioned as praying in the Gospels. Luke has eleven of them. It is evident that He loved to pray, and also, being truly Man, that He needed to pray. Let us take note of this latter point, for if He needed to pray, how much more do we need it.

Public Prayer

Think first of public prayer. How interesting it is to read of His going into the synagogue on the Sabbath Day "as His custom was" (Luke 4:16). I don't suppose things were always to His liking. I am sure He could not always approve of the preachers, but He made a point of maintaining the habit.

We sometimes find professing Christians sitting very loosely to this habit, and we only say here that their Master found it both necessary and worthwhile to go to public worship. It is "an example that ye should follow," as Peter said.

Private Prayer

In the course of ordinary life, private prayer was our Lord's habit. It occupied a great place in His life. Indeed, it was on just such an occasion that His disciples asked Him to teach them. In the passage from which our little text is taken—"as He was praying," they petitioned Him, "teach us."

In the extraordinary crises of life it was His habit: before the temptation, before choosing the twelve, at the transfiguration, in the Garden. There is no question that while He was here this was His regular habit.

Present–Day Prayer

We cannot forget His present–day prayer—"He ever liveth to make intercession for them" (Hebrews 7:25). How glorious to know that if we are among those who "come unto God by Him," we are ever being prayed for by the Divine Intercessor. If we have no one else to pray for us, He does so. If we are at times too weak and ill to pray for ourselves, He does so. What do we owe to that!

The Quiet Place

For the three and a half years of His ministry He had no fixed spot. He was homeless and was ceaselessly traveling about. Yet, He ever sought out an undisturbed place of retreat. "In a desert place," "the mountain," "a solitary place," and the nearest approach to a fixed spot, "the garden," where He "oftimes resorted"—these were the quiet oases of His fellowship with the Father. He said to us "shut thy door" (Matthew 6:), which is the same idea—the place of quiet.

Shut Off from the World

In the ordinary things of everyday life we must allow no intrusion into this sacred spot.

Shut In with God

No one else is permitted to interrupt. It is just He and we alone together for that precious period.

Shut Up to the Task

We are to give ourselves wholly to the work of prayer. That shut door, that quiet place has sometimes to be more spiritual than local—in crowded houses a believer may have to find quiet of heart while surroundings are anything but quiet! Luke 10 and John 11 and 12 give us instances of our Divine example having to discover quiet of spirit to pray in the presence of other people, and in the presence of distraction.

The Early Hour

All Hours

Our Lord used all hours for this precious purpose. No hour of the day was inappropriate. Indeed, the hours of darkness were employed at times upon the task. Three times we are told He remained all night in prayer.

Early Hours

But He had a special fondness for the early hours. You will recall the words of Mark 1:35, "And in the morning, rising up a great while before day, He went out, and departed into a solitary place, and there prayed." Some of the advantages of this were discussed earlier, advantages so rich as to stir us all to follow His example in this as in other prayer particulars. If we have difficulty in rousing ourselves to this early ministry, let us turn into a prayer the prophecy of Isaiah 50:4—"He wakeneth morning by morning."

The Intimate Approach

The Way He Began

A good beginning is a great asset in any matter—a race, a work, a speech. Anything well begun is half won. This is no less true of prayer. As we watch the Master, we note the way in which He began—"Father." This is the natural approach that He always used. We find it repeatedly in His High–Priestly prayer in John 17 as He speaks so intimately to His "Father," His "Holy Father," His "Righteous Father." How He gloried in the relationship!

We find it too in Gethsemane—"O My Father" (Matthew 26:39, 42). How trustful He was of His Father's will, and how loyally He embraced it!

The Way We Are to Begin

This is also the way in which He told us to begin: "When ye pray, say, 'Our Father'" (Luke 11:2). If we, by infinite privilege and amazing grace, have been admitted to that glorious relationship in Christ, we may use and are told to use that same intimate approach.

The Personal Note

Choosing the Twelve

The Lord, by His own example, encourages us to pray for individuals. When He chose the twelve disciples He spent the whole of the previous night in prayer. You can imagine how carefully and how tenderly He went through the list of likely candidates, and how, after consulting His Father, He made His final selection. He bore them up, one by one, before the Throne.

Choosing the One

When He chose the one disciple He reassured him of his final establishment in his faith by telling him, "I have prayed for thee" (Luke 22:32). Yes, he had been praying for Peter by name. And in that ever–living intercession that He now is carrying on, I have no doubt that our names—yours and mine—are on His lips. Wondrous thought!

The Strong Faith

We go to another occasion on which He prayed for someone by name—Lazarus. Here is a very clear example of the absolute assurance He had of prayer's answer.

Hear the Expression

Hear its expression—"Father, [note again the approach] I thank Thee that Thou hast heard me" (John 11:41). To outward appearances there was nothing whatever to justify that belief. Lazarus was still dead. But the Master knew that He had what He asked. It is a perfect illustration of Mark 11:24.

The late Dr. S.D. Gordon said, "Faith is not believing that He *can*, but that He *will*." We are not to suppose, however, that this was an isolated instance, for our Lord proceeds, "And I knew that Thou hearest Me always."

Heed the Example

Let us heed the example, for of him that does not "ask in faith," James 1:7 says, "let not that man think that He shall receive anything of the Lord." But what mighty benefits and blessings "the prayer of faith" receives (verse 15).

We could gladly go on much further in our reverent and enraptured study into the Example of prayer. In however small degree, yet in some real measure, may it be "As He . . . us."

26

The Goal

"Ask . . . that the Father may be glorified"
John 14:13

We have reserved for our last study a consideration of what is, I suppose, the kernel of the whole matter—motive! For the due discharge of spiritual responsibility, for the proper understanding of spiritual truth, for the full apprehension of spiritual experience, for the complete enjoyment of spiritual blessing, certain questions and their answers are of tremendous importance. These are questions such as What? Who? Which? Where? Whither? When? Each of them is fraught with immense significance and consequence. But perhaps more important than any of those is the further question, Why? What is the real motive of our prayer life? Why do we pray? What is our goal? To get that rightly adjusted is the supreme Prayer Secret. That is why we have left it to be dealt with late, that it may have all the emphasis of a last word.

Look to the Master's Purpose

Not Only for Ourselves

We shall say quite definitely to begin with that this is

not simply the welfare of ourselves. Note that "simply," for it is not to be assumed that to pray for our own welfare is wrong. Even our physical well-being is a proper subject of prayer, as the Master taught us when He put "Give us this day our daily bread" among the typical petitions that outline the "manner" (Matthew 6:9), in which we are to pray. Also on another occasion He included, "give us day by day our daily bread" (Luke 11:3) among the things He encouraged us to "say" when praying. What is true of material needs is no less true of spiritual necessities.

But why? How important is that "why?" One of the most common reasons for ineffectual prayer is wrong motive. "Ye ask, and receive not, because ye ask amiss, that ye may consume it upon your lusts" (James 4:3).

Not Only for Others

We state next that it is not merely the blessing of others. We add "merely" because obviously we may intercede for them. Indeed, we shall include a wide range of "others" in our supplications.

God's Glory Only

But why? Not these two purposes, simply and merely, but the glory of our God only. This is the highest purpose to which we must ever be looking in our prayers. Our own well-being and others' blessing must always subserve that great and high aim. Something might be right for us or for them, simply and merely in itself. But if, on any account, it should be not for His glory, then it should be abandoned.

Link to the Master's Purpose

Its Statement

You will note the statement of that in the completed verse of our text. It is not only what we shall "ask," but also what He will "do" that is to bring glory to God. That was ever the Master's object throughout His sojourn here—"I have glorified Thee on the earth" (John 17:4). It is His object in the ever–living "intercession for them" (Hebrews 7:25), that he is exercising at the Throne for those who "come unto God by Him."

Let us make that same purpose our own. Let the glory of the Father serve as the link between our asking and His doing. "Such prayer must prevail," says Andrew Murray.

Its Wisdom

To be joined with His purpose is an invincible thing. Abraham Lincoln once uttered this, which would be such a fine maxim for life: "Find out which way God is going, and yourself go that way." How wise that is. Study His Book to discover His plan for world affairs, spiritual affairs, dispensational affairs, personal affairs. Look out and link up.

Live Out the Same Purpose

Give heed that you are day by day living out the same purpose. There is a quite intimate connection between how we live and how we pray.

Life Conditioning Prayer

If we be sinful, there is at once a barrier between us and the Throne. "Your iniquities have separated between you and your God, and your sins have hid His face from you, that he will not hear" (Isaiah 59:2). If, on the other hand, we be holy, there is at once a sympathy between us and the Throne. If, further, we be wholly set in life upon the Father's glory, there is at once established an identity of purpose between us and the Throne. Thus does the character of our living greatly affect the efficacy of our praying.

Prayer Coloring Life

Moreover, the connection between these two things is seen to work also in the opposite direction as prayer colors life. You remember the longing of John Keble's hymn, "And help us, this and every day, To live more nearly as we pray." If the glory of the Father be, in reality, the sole source of our prayer, that will be reflected in our daily life. This would be our deepest satisfaction if people could, in however tiny a degree, allows us to say with Paul in Galatians 1:24, "They glorified God in me."

We have written much throughout these pages about the reason of our prayers. It is that God is what He is and has said what He has said. We have spoken, too, about the object of our prayers—so manifold, so far-reaching, so small, and so big.

We have not forgotten the quality of our prayers, that they should spring out of a sincere and true heart. What is more fitting than that we should have used this closing chapter to consider the motive of our prayers—the thing that we are really and ultimately aiming at. That is, not only certain things that we ask for, but that in the receiving of those things, something further may be effected. And that if that further thing would be hampered by the receiving of those nearer things, we are content, even happily content, to do without them. Anything—so long as the Further thing be advanced. The nature of that is disclosed in this study.

Let us seek grace to be able to say in uttermost sincerity that in our whole life and in our prayer life, my goal is His glory. Do you remember how the Master Himself prayed? "Father, glorify Thy name" (John 12:28). This was the goal of His prayer. So shall it be the end of ours.

Christ *Life*

MINISTRIES

"Committed to providing messages, materials, and ministries that will further revival, both personally and corporately in the local church."

Prayer Advances

Christ Life Ministries sponsors Prayer Advances for men, women, and students. These Advances are power-packed events designed to move Christians toward a meaningful relationship with God.

Spiritual Life Crusades & Prayer Summit Weekends

Evangelist Harold Vaughan travels throughout the states and foreign countries speaking in local churches and conferences.

Life Changing Resources

including audio, video, and printed materials.

GO TO **www.christlifemin.org** to learn more!

Order Form

Quantity Prices for *Prayer Secrets*

1–5 Copies $10.99 each
6–10 Copies $8.99 each
11–49 Copies $7.99 each

50–75 Copies 5.99 each
75 or More Copies 5.50 each
(Prices are subject to change.)

QTY_____ ***Prayer Secrets*** $_____

Shipping & Handling $_____

VA residents add 5% sales tax $_____

Total $_____

Shipping & Handling *(Continental USA only and subject to change)*

Under $25.00 add $5.00
$25.01–$40.00 add $6.00
$40.01–$50.00 add $7.00

$50.01–$75.00 add $8.00
Over $75.00 add 9%

NAME

ADDRESS

CITY   STATE

ZIP   PHONE

E-MAIL

❏ **Visa** ❏ **Mastercard**   **Make checks payable to: Christ Life Publications**

CARD#   EXPIRATION DATE

SIGNATURE REQUIRED

Read
The Prayer Life of Jesus
by Harold Vaughan
$6.99

Christ *Life*
PUBLICATIONS
P.O. Box 399
Vinton, VA 24179

Web site: **www.christlifemin.org**
E-mail: **info@christlifemin.org**
Phone: **(540) 890-6100**
Fax: **(540) 890-4133**